THIS THING

CALLED

YOU

Ernest Holmes

For information regarding special discounts for bulk purchases, please contact BN Publishing at info@bnpublishing.com

©**Copyright 2007 – BN Publishing**
www.bnpublishing.com

ALL RIGHTS RESERVED
Printed in the U.S.A.

© Copyright 2007 – BN Publishing

Table of Contents

Chapter I

YOU, LIKE all others, are seeking the joy of living. You wish to be needed, to be loved, to be included in the great drama of life. This urge is in every individual. It is in everything. The rose exists to express beauty. Root and branch conspire with nature to give birth to blossom. An artist will starve in his garret that he may chisel an angelic form from a slab of marble, compelling the unyielding substance to accept his breath of creation.

Not only human beings but everything in nature is endowed with this creative urge. When moisture is precipitated, the desert receives it with gladness and breaks forth into a song of creation. Making the most of its brief season, it blossoms in joy, storing within its bosom the seed of a future flowering. It is impossible to escape this creative urge. Everything must find fulfillment or perish.

No man willed this so. Evolution is proof of an irresistible urge which pushes everything onward and upward. Man did not create life; he is something that lives in, from, and by it. He cannot escape life or the necessity of giving expression to it through living.

In some way which you know not of, through some process which never reveals its face, Life has entered into you and with it the irresistible impulse to create. Divine Intelligence has willed it so; nor you, nor any other person, nor all the wit, science or philosophy of man, nor the inspiration of saints or sages, can change one bit of it any more than man can arrest the eternal circuits of time, the revolutions of the planets or the desire of the fledgling to leave its nest, to soar and sing.

Create or perish is the eternal mandate of nature. Be constructive or become frustrated, is an equal demand. You cannot escape the conclusion that whatever this thing is which is seeking expression through everything, it can find satisfactory outlet only through constructive and life-giving creativeness. You may call this process good or evil, right or wrong, God or the devil, heaven or hell. Would it not be more simple to say that finally things work out for the best only when they are life-giving?

We are all some part of a universal order. The very urge for personal gratification is incomplete until it finds a universal outlet. This is the cause back of all upheavals in human history. The pattern is trying to fit the pieces into greater and greater units as though it could not accomplish its purpose through anything other than a democracy of Spirit, a union of all. This union, however, does not mean sameness, for while unity requires conformity to principles, unity never means uniformity. Every blade of grass, every crystal, every drop of water, like every individual, is a little different from any other one of its species.

Humanity is made up of innumerable individuals, no two alike, and yet society is a composite whole moving gradually toward some ultimate goal. What could this goal be other than that everyone, while remaining individual, shall find a more complete expression in and among all other individuals?

You belong to the universe in which you live, you are one with the Creative Genius back of this vast array of ceaseless motion, this original flow of life. You are as much a part of it as the sun, the earth and the air. There is something in you telling you this—like a voice echoing from some mountain top of inward vision, like a light whose origin no man has seen, like an impulse welling up from an invisible source.

Your soul belongs to the universe. Your mind is an outlet through which the Creative Intelligence of the universe seeks fulfillment.

This is your starting point for investigating the meaning of those impulses, longings, and desires which accompany you through life. You may accept that the source through which they come is real. You may accept that the universe is filled with a Divine and Infinite Presence, perhaps the infinite of yourself. Not the infinite of your limited self, but the infinite of the Divine Self you must be. There must be a pattern of yourself in this invisible.

The greatest minds of the ages have accepted that such a pattern exists. Socrates called it his spirit. Some ancient mystics called it Atman. Why don't you call it just you, your complete self? For surely this is what they all have meant.

Just try to catch the larger vision and realize that there have been and are people, many of them, who have wooed and wed some invisible Presence until Its atmosphere and essence have become woven into the fabric of their own existence. Every man is a doorway, as Emerson said, through which the Infinite passes into the finite, through which God becomes man, through which the Universal becomes individual.

You are to believe with utmost simplicity and with complete faith that there is a pattern of your being, or a real spirit of you, which is as eternal as God, as indestructible as Reality, and as changeless as Truth. This pattern is seeking to manifest through you. Back of it is all the will and purpose of the universe, all the irresistible laws of being. Finally it will win.

It is because it is there that you have these irresistible urges—the longing to live more fully, the feeling that life belongs to you. There is something within you beyond all doubt and fear, something which has never been limited by your acts or destroyed by your feeling. This is the only something that can make you whole.

Chapter II

WHY, THEN, if these things are true, is the world still impoverished, mentally and physically ill, and apparently unable to become unified? This is the great question—Why, and Why, and Why? Unless this question is adequately answered and its meaning increasingly applied to human conduct, there is danger that the world may destroy its vast system of misconceptions and be compelled to begin over again.

It seems as though a persistent purpose were being carried out, that anything which does not comply with this purpose must become submerged in the backwash of evolution, that that which is more nearly right may come forward. The world has reached a dramatic climax in its history. It has unlocked so much of the physical resources of the universe that unless this enormous power is used constructively it can well destroy it. The world stands on the brink of a great abyss, a terrific regression, or, if it chooses, faces the horizon of a glorious day, a new age.

But you may ask, "Why would an Almighty Power and a Divine Intelligence permit such possible disaster?" This is something that you and I have no control over. God, or the Creative Genius of the universe, has placed this prerogative in the mind of man through giving him volition and choice. God Himself could not will it otherwise. For, if there is to be a valid choice, it must be accompanied by the possibility of more than one thing to choose.

This is what Moses meant when he said that the word is in your own mouth —a blessing or a curse according to the way you use it. You want Life to live through you. You want joy to express itself in you. You desire peace of mind and happiness, success, health, radiant living. How could you desire these things unless they already exist as possibilities? Is there not an echo within you, as though it came from some invisible source—a deep feeling, an intuitive something? You cannot quite put it into words, yet there it is, definite as your life.

Do not be afraid of this urging. All nature obeys it blindly. The culminating and triumphant result of evolution has placed in you the possibility of accepting or rejecting. In wonder and awe before the grandeur of this possibility the mind stands still, the imagination is staggered, but that hope which springs perennial in man's consciousness says, "Beloved, now are we the sons of God, and it doth not yet appear what we shall be: but we know that, when he shall appear, we shall be like him; for we shall see him as he is."

Chapter II

You already are a spiritual being. When the mind understands this and embodies its essence, that which you are in the invisible will become more apparent in the visible. You have concluded that this is true. You are reinforced by the wisdom of the ages and are rapidly becoming further reinforced through scientific investigation. Let us see if we cannot discover what blocks the way. We shall not discover any block in Reality Itself, but in our attitude toward It. Now that man has reached the stage of self-choice he can temporarily, but not permanently, block the Divine intention.

Browning said that man can desecrate but never lose the divine spark. It is always there. "I am with you always, even unto the end of the world." Let us suppose that you are spirit, soul and body, as the Bible states; that your spirit already is perfect, an individualized center in the consciousness of God. God has made you out of Himself. The only material He had was the Substance of His own being. The only mind He had to implant in you was His Mind. The only spirit He had to impart was His own Spirit.

You are a living being by virtue of the fact that through some process which no man knows, needs to know, or can know, Life is incarnated in you, operating through you this moment. This is the gift of Life.

But you are an individual, like all other individuals gradually awakening to the greater possibility. If Life made you out of Itself, which It most certainly did, and if you are an individual just a little different from all other individuals who ever lived, then Life not only created you as an independent being, It also implanted a unique something within you. It will never be duplicated. The spirit that accompanies you through your life is just a little different from the spirit of any other person—not different in that it is isolated, because all are rooted in one being, but different in that it is individual.

Suppose you were to think of it this way: there is a spirit in me and this spirit is God as His own son. Whether or not I understand it, there is a real Myself which forever exists in pure Spirit. I had nothing to do with this. I merely awoke and discovered it. I did not give it to myself, and I cannot withdraw myself from it. I can only accept it.

Since you are an individual you can either accept or reject your own spirit. Of course, no one can take it away from you. Somewhere along the line you will be compelled to accept it. However, you can procrastinate, you can divert, you can sidestep or delay this divine event. If you knew beyond question that this is true, your greatest search would be after your own spirit. Well, you do know this. Every desire you have for betterment in life is some echo from that deep within which forevermore proclaims, "Behold, I make all things new."

It is because your mind has the prerogative of accepting or rejecting that the Bible states: "Behold, I stand at the door, and knock: If any man hear my voice, and open the door, I will come in and sup with him, and he with me." Suppose, with utmost simplicity, you accept the spirit that is in you—not in the mountain, not at Jerusalem, not even in the temple, although it is there also, but in you—the spirit of yourself. Standing between this spirit, your physical body and external affairs, there is the sum total of your thinking, believing, and feeling.

Perhaps, more than anyone understands or believes, the sum total of every man's thought is a mirage of the ages. It would be well to think of it this way that you may not condemn yourself. You are like everyone else, "an infant crying in the night"—something trying to be made whole, something with a deep yearning for security, a deep and unspeakable longing for love, for protection and for peace.

But the mind is filled with the accumulated doubts of the ages, as though a vast abyss of doubt, fear and uncertainty were standing between you and your desires. Here is where Science of Mind can aid you, where your intellect may reach through to unite with your inspiration, where the conscious use of the laws of mind may break down the barriers which hide the face of love from the fact of unloveliness.

If God created you after His own nature (and there is nothing else He could have made you out of) then the thing you are after is already here, within you. The only things that stand between you and it are the accumulated thoughts, beliefs and emotions of the ages. But there is nothing there that has not been put there either by yourself or the race. What has been put there can be removed. These unbeliefs are thought patterns laid down throughout the ages and accentuated by your own experience, by your inherited tendencies and environment. There is no use wasting time speculating as to what avenue they came through. Your job is to reject them.

Your intellect has now accepted that you can do this. Are you not, then, like one who has started on a journey to a beautiful city which he knows exists? What if he has to climb a few mountains, make a certain number of detours, and cross a desert or ford a stream? Everything that is worth attaining is worth striving toward. It is the goal you are after. You have a vision and you are going to follow it.

You may not reach your city of good in a single day, but its image out there in your desert is not a mirage. There was never a counterfeit without a reality back of it. Fortunately, your destiny is not external. If it were you could not reach your goal. One by one, without frenzy or impatience, you are going to remove the mental blocks that stand between you and your destiny. What thought has done, thought can undo. The mental patterns laid down in your subconscious throughout the ages can be consciously removed.

This great thing within you, which is called will or choice, can decide your destiny. It can remove every obstruction and gradually implant new patterns in your mind.

Suppose you look at the proposition from another viewpoint. Suppose you place your physical environment, including your body and your conscious mind, at one end of a line. At the other end place your spiritual being, God and infinite possibility. At this end of the line everything is already perfect. This is called the Kingdom of Heaven on earth. It should make its advent in your experience. It wants to.

This end of the line is the Kingdom which has been promised. This Spirit is happy, whole, free, filled with joy, eternal in Its existence, and can provide you with everlasting expansion. All your highest hopes and dreams have come from It. The echo of Its being is in your intellect, the voice of Its unspoken word is in your mind, the feeling of Its light and life is in your heart, the emotion of Its imagination is in your soul.

At the other end of the line is your physical environment, including your body, most of your conscious thoughts, your daily hopes and aspirations, fears and failures. All apparently isolated, wandering in a desert of despair, climbing endless mountains, at times lost in interminable forests through which light does not break, fording rushing streams in the turmoil of life— searching, wondering, hoping, longing, yearning toward that other half of its being which alone can make it whole.

Don't you think this is a good description of your attitudes and experiences? One-half of you in heaven, the other half on a dense earth; the heavenly willing to come forward and answer your every need, the earthly-half striving toward the heavenly—and the apparent barrier. If you knew, as you know that you live, that this barrier were only a thing of thought or belief, the first half of your journey would be accomplished. You would know that you have the tools to cut down the forests, level the mountains, bridge the streams and cause the desert to bloom.

If you listen to yourself long enough you will know this. With hope and enthusiasm you will start on your journey. You will never become discouraged or disheartened. Your vision will be on this city of good and your feet, your mind, your intellect, your will, will travel toward this city and you shall surely enter its gates.

Let us use another illustration. Let us think of a tunnel, one end of which is out in the open where there are fertile valleys, glorious sunshine, verdant vegetation. There is song, laughter, happiness, peace and joy. Let us call this the Valley of Contentment. Let us also call it the Kingdom of God.

You are at the other end of this tunnel in a deep, dark cavern, overlooking a desert through which no refreshing streams flow. Somehow your attention has been drawn to the open end of this tunnel. With a curiosity that you did not put in your mind, you wish to investigate where this tunnel leads, what is at the other end of it. You peer into the tunnel. At first it seems dark, but occasionally a shaft of light shines through it and you catch a vision of the other side.

You have a great longing to walk through this tunnel, to leave behind the dismal scene of discontent and unhappiness, and to enter into the joy that your brief glimpse has promised. For in this glimpse you have seemed to see yourself standing at the other end of the tunnel. Perhaps, in this momentary vision you seem to have seen your own spirit. It seems as though something says, "Yes, this is myself. How am I going to unite myself with myself?" Then darkness closes in. Your vision has vanished. It must have been an illusion.

Now there are two voices that seem to be talking to you. One voice says, "You are following a mirage, an illusion. There is nothing real but this end of the tunnel. Accept things as they are. Make the best of them. Be as happy as you can, but do not hope." This is the voice of despair. The other voice is saying, "Do not be afraid. Your vision is true. Enter the tunnel and walk through. There is nothing solid in it. That which obstructs your passage is vapor, the vapor of unbelief. It is dense only with the denseness of doubt. It is filled with the thoughts of the ages. There is a lamp within you already lighted. As you walk through the tunnel the darkness will disappear because of this light. You will find that other half of yourself and you will discover that this tunnel is your own mind."

This is a picture of yourself—your efforts, your hopes and longings, your inspirations and doubts, your fears and faiths.

The barriers between you and your greater good are not barriers in themselves. They are things of thought. It is because of this that all things are possible to faith. "It is done unto you as you believe." In interpreting this saying you must pause after the word as. Think about its meaning and you will discover that it is saying that life not only responds to your belief, it responds after the manner of your believing, as you believe. It is a mirror reflecting the image of your belief.

While the laws of mind, like all laws of nature, are neutral, good must finally overcome evil. Evil is a negation. Good is positive. Like light and darkness—darkness cannot overcome light, but light can neutralize darkness. And in this good is included all things in this life that make for full livingness and joy, peace and happiness, health and harmony, and the success that rightfully belongs to a Divine Being.

The only warning made against the use of this highest law of your being was that it should not be used destructively, "…for all they that take the sword shall perish with the sword." The Kingdom of God contains everything that is or could be desirable. This everything already exists as a potential something to be drawn upon. You may use this potential for any good purpose, not only with certainty of success but with safety. It is only when we use natural forces wrongly that they can destroy, and it is ordained that this destruction be of a temporary nature.

You wish to use the laws of your being in such a way that they cannot bring evil to yourself or others. Therefore, you must be certain that your desire is toward more life for everyone, including yourself. If you follow this rule you cannot use the law wrongly.

There is a law of faith and belief, which is just as definite as any other law in nature. This law utilizes the Creative Principle of Life in such a way that all lesser uses of It become submerged. This is the triumph of Spirit.

Chapter III

"IT IS done unto you as you believe", implies that there is a law which operates upon your faith. All laws are universal, hence they exist wherever you are. If there is a law of faith, it is right where you are and it will operate like any other law in nature.

For instance, it will work like the law of gravitation, which automatically holds everything in place. But so far as you are concerned, it will hold things where you place them. You do not change the law of gravitation, you merely change your position in it. This law works automatically. As you shift objects around in the position that seems desirable to you, it will hold them there. This law works for you on the scale of your own individual being.

Suppose you want to change the position of the furniture in your room. You move the piano from one place to another. This is an act of volition on your part. Perhaps you wish to move the stove into the living room. This might seem an eccentric act but the law does not question it. It will automatically hold things where you place them; it will operate upon your decision.

The law of faith acts on your belief. And now comes the more subtle and interesting part of this story, which perhaps you have not analyzed. At the expense of repetition let us look into this a little more carefully, because it is of such importance. It is this little word as that you are to consider the meaning of. Not only is there a law which does something for you (this is easy enough to accept), but in doing so it is limited to your belief. This is the important thing to remember.

It is only common sense to recognize that what this law does for you it must, of necessity, do through you. The gift of Life is not complete until it is accepted. If you can believe only in a little good, then the law will be compelled to operate on that little good. Not that the law of itself knows anything about big and little any more than the law of gravitation would know that a mountain is heavier than a marble—it automatically holds everything in place. If you remove a large pile of gravel it will hold this bulk in place. If you dip up but a few thimblefuls it will hold this smaller amount in place with equal impartiality.

Now, shift this whole proposition over into the mental plane, realizing that the mental reproduces the physical, but at a higher level. The law is always a mirror reflecting your mental attitudes. Therefore, if you say, "I can have a little good," it will produce this small amount of good for you, but if you say, "All the good there is mine," with equal certainty it will produce a larger good. If you believe that wherever you go you will meet with love and friendship, with appreciation and gratitude, then this will become the law of your life.

The late Dr. Carrel said that faith operates on its plane as physical laws operate on their plane, reproducing the same action at a higher level. He was careful to explain that the laws of faith do not destroy physical laws. One law of God could not destroy another. Spiritual laws reproduce physical laws at a higher level. The higher law automatically controls the lower. This is equal to saying that the laws of mind can be made to control the physical body and the physical environment when they are rightly used, not through denying body or environment, but by including them in a larger system.

This is what faith does. You should think of the law of faith just as naturally as you would any other law in nature. Faith does not obliterate other laws, nor can faith which is not true create truth out of error; rather, faith in right must always reverse that which is wrong. So far no one has disproved this theory. All who have acted upon it have received a definite result. Faith is a great adventure, a stimulating pursuit, a worthwhile attempt to utilize the higher laws of your being for definite purposes.

The law of faith operates with integrity on the definite idea, thought, expectancy or acceptance implanted. But the seed must be left in the creative soil of mind until it can mature. There is a time for sowing as well as a time for harvest. Plants must not be pulled up or interrupted in the process of their growth. They must be watered with hope, fertilized with expectancy and cultivated with enthusiasm, gratitude, and joyous recognition.

If the law operates automatically, then you do not coerce, concentrate or compel it. You provide mental attitudes which it may operate upon. You do not hold the law in place, you hold your ideas in place. This is your individual effort. Your concentration is not on the law, because that is already here, it is right where you are, it is within you as well as around you. This concentration is not coercion but a good-natured flexibility with yourself, gradually eliminating doubt, fear and uncertainty, and replacing them with certainty, assurance, recognition and gratitude.

This process is not so much a problem of will as it is one of willingness. The only important role the will plays is in a decision to keep thought poised long enough to permit the law to operate. This is not a prayer of beseechment but a recognition or acknowledgment of right action.

Faith is the most important thing in your life. It is impossible to arrive at the grandeur of its possibility through petty thinking and small ideas. The whole mental scope must be broadened and deepened, the whole expectancy must reach out to more, the whole imagination must lend its feeling to grateful acceptance and joyous recognition.

All thoughts of suffering for righteousness' sake, all beliefs that you are being tempted or tried to see if you are worthy of the gifts of Life, are mistaken concepts of the way this law works. Life wishes to make the gift because in so doing It is flowing into Its own self-expression. You might say that gravity wishes to hold an object in place because this is its nature. As a matter of fact, it cannot help doing so. But if you place the gas range in the living room and keep it lighted on a hot summer day you will be uncomfortable. If you place it too close to the draperies no doubt they will catch fire.

This does not mean that the law would have any evil intent. You could as well put the range in the rear garden. You might put an electric heater in your icebox and the ice would melt, not because the law wishes to destroy the contents of the box, but because laws are always impersonal. Hence, since there is a law of belief, of necessity you must always be using it; being individuals with free will you must expect to reap as you have sown.

You wish to reap joy, happiness, love, friendship, health, harmony and success. Could you expect to keep your mind filled with such thoughts for yourself unless it were filled with similar thoughts for others? Of course not. This would not make sense. Therefore, the Bible commands us to be kind to everyone; "give and to you shall be given." Moreover, when you give, the gift will return to you multiplied. What a marvelous concept this is! It seems too good to be true. Yet plant a seed in the ground and it multiplies its own type many times.

There is a law of multiplicity in nature. You have a right to expect that what you wish for others will be returned to you through others. You have no right to expect that you can reap where you have not sown.

This is one of the great laws of cause and effect, laws that produce justice without judgment—the inevitable result of laws that work with mathematical certainty. You cannot love and hate at the same time, nor can anyone else. All the poetry, wit, knowledge and art of the ages cannot alter the fact that love alone begets love, peace alone attracts peace, only that which goes forth in joy can return with gladness—give and to you shall be given, and the type multiplied, good measure, running over and pressed down.

You need not force or coerce, but you must obey the law. If you can see God in everything, then God will look back at you through everything. This is the meaning of that saying: "Act as though I am, and I will be." This is the law of

19

give and take.

When the time comes that nothing goes forth from you other than that which you would be glad to have return, then you will have reached your heaven.

Chapter IV

THE UNIVERSE is one vast system. All the laws of nature conspire to benefit mankind, but these same laws automatically protect the integrity of nature. It is as though nature said, "All right, little man, the game is yours. Play it as you see fit. I am going to serve you, but don't fool yourself. I am going to reflect right back to you with exactness what you really are. If you don't like what is happening, I am not going to be disturbed. You are the arbiter of your fate. You are the captain of your soul.

"I have given you all. I have implanted freedom, individuality and self-choice within you. Finally, through experience you will learn the better and wiser way. I am love as well as law, beauty as well as reason, feeling as well as intellect. You are set on the path of self-determination. Your fantastic will, seeking good for yourself that you would not willingly give to others, may lead you up many blind alleys, you may meet with disappointment and chagrin, but I have also placed within you a compass and a chart. There is a course you may pursue which leads to happiness, to wholeness, to peace of mind and joy.

"Some day you will follow this path, because I have placed a spirit within you which is ever seeking to guide, ever standing aside permitting you partially to obliterate that spark which is part of Myself. Through all the rounds of experience I am there.

"Some day when you sit down by the roadside, weary with struggle, you will listen deeply and you will hear a voice saying, 'This is the path, follow it.' Even then I shall wait, for you are you and you cannot return to your Father's house other than as a complete and perfect individualization of Myself. Always I shall be waiting. I shall not reproach you when you return. You will be welcome. The time of your return is in your own decision. It may be now or at any time in that vast forever which stretches before you."

The freedom which the all-creative Wisdom has designed for man is marvelous beyond human perception. Life has given man an intuitive sense of things; it has permitted him to evolve through countless ages of trial and error to the day of his redemption, always knowing that this redemption is certain. But the timing, even of eternity, so far as man is concerned, rests in his present or delayed acceptance. It could be today or tomorrow. It could have been yesterday. We are living in a universal now and this now waits on our acceptance.

Many people naturally ask, "If God is good, if God is love, if God is peace, why all this confusion?" Don't you think that even God could not have done it any other way? Can't you see that even the Divine Will, in ordaining man's destiny, was compelled to let man work out his own future?

The more you think about this proposition, the clearer it will become. Do you think it would have been possible for it to have been any other way? You would not wish to be an automaton any more than would wish to be a cabbage or a wave of the ocean or a knot in a tree. The greatest gift Life could have made to you is yourself. You are a spontaneous, self-choosing center in Life, in the great drama of being, the great joy of becoming, the certainty of eternal expansion. You could not ask for more and more could not have been given.

Life will be to you what you are to It. Of necessity there is a Divine Pattern at the center of everything. This is the God in you waiting your recognition. Somehow, you must link your will, your thought, your intellect, your imagination and your feeling with the Divine Presence which is already there. Between this perfection and completion, which already exists, and your intellect, environment and everyday experience, there is the accumulated experience of your subconscious mind.

In reality there is no such thing as your subconscious mind, for what the analyst analyzes and the psychologist psychologizes is not another mind, it is merely the accumulated thought and feeling of the ages operating through you. It is no more a mind apart or separate than the law of gravitation, which holds you to the earth, is an individual law. All laws are universal and may become individualized. The thing that stands between you and the greater good is a thing of thought and nothing else. It is not Reality that you must change, but your mental reaction to It.

What is called the subjective state of your thought, the accumulated patterns, is automatically attracting or repelling. These patterns are automatically resowing their own seeds in the creative medium of mind. They will keep on doing this until you change them. They will do this without volition of your intellect.

Your hope lies in the fact that you can change these patterns. Perhaps not in a moment or a day, or a month or a year, but you can change them. This is not a process of merely making affirmations or holding thoughts, it is a process of the gradual re-education of your whole mental reaction. It is a process of following the intuition back to the pattern, of feeling toward it, of accepting it, and of acting as though it were there.

The whole thing is so simple that at first it seems impossible that it could be that way, yet it is. As you watch your mental actions and reactions, particularly those that are rooted in feeling, as you observe your expectations, you will feel impulses rising from within—habits of belief, patterns of thought— too many of which are negative.

As you carefully weigh and measure the operation of this unconscious expectancy as it comes to the surface, you can detect what has to be changed. If you can accept that these impulsions are thought patterns that have been laid down there by yourself or the sum total of human belief, you will realize that they can be changed by bringing in exactly opposite thought patterns. This will not be a question of struggling with the old patterns so much as it will be one of gradually straining them out.

You will notice, if you follow a few simple rules and methods carefully, that when thoughts of confusion persist in coming to the surface, statements of peace will neutralize them. When thoughts of fear assail, statements of faith will counteract their action. When thoughts of unhappiness well up from within, thoughts of happiness and joy will transmute them through the alchemy of Spirit.

First of all you must arrive at peace of mind. It is only on the basis of peace that you can persist with absolute certainty. Peace alone gives poise. There is an intuition within you which already knows that you are one with good, that your destiny is certain, and you must listen to this intuition for it is the voice of God in you.

Quite naturally, many ask, "Is there a secret way? Is there an occult way? Is there some great thing that only a few people know, the great and wise ones, that I must learn? Must I fast, concentrate and pray without ceasing? Must I beseech or implore? Must I work out all the mistakes I have ever made to become redeemed? Must I renounce everything to find peace? How am I going to be made whole?"

Unfortunately, many persons labor under the mistaken idea that there are deep secrets, that there are subtle and unknown pathways which a few people know about, great truths which only a few have realized, and so the search goes on through the pathway of mystery. Many persons sincerely believe that every mistake they have made will be held against them for an indefinite period. Many others believe that God is trying them, and far too many believe in the necessity of devious pathways, strange and weird rites, adherence to certain forms and rituals.

You are to take a more direct and simple path from your intellect to your true self. Not withholding from any other his way (which no doubt is good for him), you are to become a simple and direct soul. The answer is not in any book but in yourself.

The time of redemption is not something stretching out through endless incarnations or equally endless purgatories. Your kingdom is at hand, the eleventh hour is not too late, and the time of your redemption is that split second when the sum total of your thinking includes that which belongs to the kingdom of good.

When the first house was lighted with electricity, the darkness did not groan and say, "How long have I been dark. How ignorant have been those who have permitted this darkness. What grievous mistakes they have made." The darkness said nothing when the light spoke; and the light shown in that darkness and the darkness was not. There were no devious paths other than the discovery of the light. There was no judgment of darkness against the light. There was no action of darkness upon the light. The light merely exclaimed, "Behold, I come!" and the darkness disappeared.

The eternal Giver is equally the eternal Forgiver, and love forever counterbalances hate. Joy will always put sadness to flight and good will overcome evil. Peace will neutralize confusion, and hope will banish doubt. Could anything be more simple? Do not delay your good by thinking that you have so much evil to overcome.

The universe is made up of love and law. God is love. Love is givingness; love is also for givingness. There is a law of cause and effect which automatically compels man to reap as he sows. The day he ceases to sow error he will begin to reap truth. When he stops sowing hate he will reap love. When he stops sowing unforgivingness he will be forgiven. When he stops sowing fear he will reap faith.

There is no mystery here. Simple, direct statements of cause and effect—the inevitable necessity of good finally overcoming evil, the glorious concept that the Kingdom of God, in all its wonder and beauty, exists eternally, changelessly, waiting your recognition.

Since you are primarily a spiritual and mental being, you must rearrange your thoughts to meet, to agree with, to harmonize and unify with this new concept. No one can do this for you as well as you can do it for yourself. Try to simplify the whole process, make it direct. You are starting out on a great adventure, a wonderful journey. You are guided by love, inspired by truth, and your future will be what you make it.

Chapter V

IT IS wonderful to know that your good is at hand. Your night wanes. Your dawn is breaking. There is a living Spirit at the center of your being. The original Author of all life is in and around you—not a God who was, but a God who is. This is the great secret which you share with Life. Life is wherever you are. It revolves around you even as It flows through you. Keep the doorway of your mind open. Feeling, thinking, communing with this Life, know that It fills you with light and with power.

Learn to exchange fears, doubts and uncertainties for faith. Faith can make you whole. Faith can convert fear into certainty, poverty into riches, disease into health. Faith can lift you from a valley of despair into a mountain of hope and certainty. There is a power which flows out through your words of faith. There is a law of faith which has the power to bring into your life everything you need.

You need not go through any practices to unify with this Power, for you are already one with It. You need not go in search of It because It is already where you are. Because you are always in contact with It, you can bring into your life the good you so greatly desire, for It will honor your desires. It will bring them into manifestation in your life. Say to yourself, then:

I place my affairs in the hands of goodness, love and wisdom.
I place them there with supreme confidence.
I have a childlike faith and trust in good.
I know there is nothing between me and that which is best.
I am filled with enthusiastic hope.
I look forward to entering into the fullness of life.

The greatest adventure of your life lies in your conscious use of this power. You need not believe in any particular religious system to discover the wellspring of life. You find it at the center of your own being, in the quiet of the evening, in the stillness of the night, at the dawn of the new day, and in the midst of activity.

Nothing can be more immediate or personal to you than this Presence which is in everything, and without which there could be neither life, thought nor action. Accept this here and now, today. Say:

I am conscious that good is expressing through my thought.
My mind is open to the influx of truth.
I am guided.

I am informed. I am guarded.

I am led into pathways of peace and goodness.

You need not mold your life after another. Trust yourself. Believe in your direct relationship with Life and you will not be disappointed. Do not wait. Today is the time to start. Right where you are is the place to begin.

Electricity exists everywhere but its energy must be directed. So it is with this Power. If you wish It to pour out through your thought in any direction you wish, you must use it consciously. You do not pray this Power into existence. Your use of It is not a prayer to the Power but a recognition of It. This is not a petition but a performance. Say:

I realize the presence of the living Spirit within me.

My physical body is formed of spiritual substance.

It is divinely conceived and perfectly created.

There is perfect co-ordination in every part of my being because the Spirit of perfection is acting in and through me.

To realize that God is ever-present, ever-available, is to know that all the wisdom, intelligence and power of the universe is right where you are. Your word is power when you know this. This is why everything in your life depends upon your belief, why it is done unto you as you believe. Change your belief and you can change your world.

Don't let anyone tell you this isn't true. Those who have used it in the right way have proved it to be true. Those who have never tried it know nothing about it. Don't argue with them. Let them alone.

The answers to your problems lie not in God's willingness but in your ability to believe. Certain statements repeated over and over help you to believe. Gradually these statements sink into consciousness, changing your mental reactions from negative to positive. Say:

The Law of Good is continuously operative in my life.

I am always equal to any task set before me.

I am confident of my ability to meet every situation.

I can solve every problem, overcome every difficulty.

Realizing that Spirit knows no obstruction, I have implicit confidence in Its ability to operate through me always, and under every situation.

When you use the word "God" you mean the Power that creates everything, that gives life to everything. When you say, "All things are possible," you mean that the Power which created the planets is now operating in your affairs, in and through everything you do. Your faith in It clears your mind of fear and uncertainty, and provides a channel through which the Power may work for you. There is nothing this Power cannot do for you if you learn how to use It. It is impossible for It to fail. All failure is of man. None comes from God.

It is a known fact that thoughts, often repeated, form patterns in mind which automatically reproduce themselves. This is one of the basic principles of the new knowledge of the mind. This illustration is often used by psychologists to explain continuously repeated neurotic conditions. Why not use this creative law constructively, dislodging old thought patterns with their morbid reactions to life? These thought patterns have hypnotized humanity into the belief that fear, unhappiness, poverty and sickness must prevail. Why not disrobe this mental darkness with the glorious conception of the new light, now known to exist? Say:

My mind is open to new ideas.

The Spirit is ever active in me.

The Divine Mind is inexhaustible.

There is no weary or monotonous action in Spirit. It is forever new and vibrant, fresh with ideas.

I know that I am continuously receiving new impressions from Life—new, better and fuller ways of living. I let the newness, freshness and originality of Spirit permeate my entire consciousness.

If you would exchange joy for tears, forget the tears and turn to joy. Change your mental pictures and thus create new experiences. You must not only realize that God is right where you are, you must also know that the Law of God responds to you. Say:

I sense my oneness with all life.

I enter into the joy of conscious union with the Infinite.

There is One Mind, this Mind is God; this Mind is my mind now.

Chapter V

I am conscious of Infinite Peace, Divine Joy and Complete Security.

Spirit is at the center of everything. It is the center of all personality. As a drop of water is in the ocean, so you are in an ocean of Life. This Life acts as law upon your thought.

Perhaps this seems too good to be true. Remember, however, that the first steam-driven ship to cross the ocean carried in her cabin a book carefully explaining just why it was that a boat could not be driven by steam. A new energy is now being announced to the world—the creative power of thought which draws its energy from a universal source.

Your consciousness, which means the sum total of your thoughts, is the medium between the invisible Cause and your personal life. Though you were in hell and you dwelt on heavenly things, you would immediately find yourself in heaven. Though you were in heaven and dwelt on evil, you would immediately find yourself in hell. Evil is the result of a wrong use of the Law of Life. Therefore, your greatest desire should be to use this Law rightly. You always use it rightly when you use it constructively. You use it constructively when there is nothing in you that would hurt anyone. You use it constructively when you use it with love.

It is not necessary to spend your entire time in prayer and meditation. Rather, seek to make your work a prayer, your believing an act, your living an art. It is then that the object of your faith will be made visible to you. It is then that you shall "kiss the lips of your desire."

Your thought is creative, not because you will, wish, hope, pray or long for it to be so. It is creative because there is a creative law operating upon it. You did not make this law; you only use it. Say:

My affairs are in the keeping of Infinite Wisdom.

I am guided by Divine Intelligence.

The activity of Spirit inspires my mind and flows through my actions.

Life lies open to me, rich, full and abundant.

It is important that you maintain a strict censorship over your thinking. Just as you watch your garden that foreign seeds shall not fall into it, producing a growth of undesirable plants, so you must refuse entrance to any thoughts you do not wish to see manifested in your life.

Guard well this garden of your mind. It is God's garden of your soul. It is your Garden of Eden wherein may grow your fondest desires and hopes, blossoming into fulfillment. Or, if you permit, the weeds of destruction, fear and doubt, will choke out the beauty of hope until despair alone remains.

Chapter V

Watch carefully, then, this garden of your soul. Plant there only seeds of happiness, of joy, of peace and of good will.

It may be necessary to cultivate your garden, to uproot the weeds and straighten out the rows, planting new seeds—new ideas, broader visions and deeper realizations of life. New aspirations must be bedded here, fertilized with the fervor of hope, the conviction of faith, the beauty of wholeness and the quietness of peace. Watch your garden carefully, guard it patiently, waiting for a new harvest—for you shall reap what you have sown.

Plant love in your garden. Kindness and sympathy flow from the heart of love, and human goodness follows divine realization at every turn in life's road. Kindness and understanding are divine flames lighted from the altar of love, upon which burns the Light Eternal.

Go often into your garden. Sitting under the Tree of Life in cool, quiet communion, you will find fresh inspiration. God Himself will go forth anew into creation through you.

The Power of the Spirit, which is ever with you, is sufficient to meet your every need. If you need healing, this Power can heal you. If you need happiness, the Spirit can provide it. If you need supply, the God who is ever with you can give it. No matter what situation you may be in, it can be changed. The winds of God never cease to blow. Set the sails of your hope that these winds may fill them. Learn to drink freely from the fountain of Life.

It may seem strange that the law which now holds you in bondage can as easily give you freedom. But this is the truth. There cannot be two final powers in the universe. If there were, one would destroy the other. There is only One Power—use It!

In such degree as your thought has a preponderance of successful feeling, your living will become successful. The Law of Life can work for you only as it works through your thought patterns. Since it is possible to control your thoughts, it is possible to control your destiny. Say:

I am a free soul.

I am completely, positively and eternally free.

I am free from doubt, fear or unhappiness, today and forever.

Chapter VI

SPIRIT WITHHOLDS nothing from you. To believe that God refuses the good you desire is to deny the goodness of God. It is a refusal to accept the profound conclusion of the one who said, "It is done unto you as you believe."

Often you may find that even though you start with an enthusiastic conviction, you become stranded on the rock of unbelief. Refuse to let this discourage you. The law still is that it is done unto you as you believe. No matter how subtle the thoughts of lack, fear, uncertainty or loneliness may be, they do not belong to you. Your affirmation can erase them. Become master of your thinking, hence master of your fate.

Always do this with a sense of union with good, for you have not been left alone to fight a losing battle or contend against powers of evil. You have been left alone to discover your real nature, that as an individual you may consciously unite with the Law of Life and the Presence of Good.

Be persistent. Keep on knocking at the doorway of your consciousness until every "no" becomes a "yes", every negation an affirmation, every fear a faith. You cannot fail if you remain steadfast. Finally, the fetters of bondage will drop from you. You will walk out of your self-imposed prison only to discover that the door was never really locked and the windows were not actually barred. You were bound merely by chains of unbelief.

If you listen to peace you will experience it. If you listen for truth you will hear it. If you listen to power you will receive it. If you listen to wholeness you will discover it.

The creative law which you use is like a mirror. The thought you hold before it is like an image. The mirror reflects the image you hold before it. Hold there, then, the image of faith and expectancy with enthusiastic conviction and with undying trust. The only thing that can hinder you is yourself. The only thing that can help you is yourself. Because it is you who reflects the image in the mirror.

Often, good and sincere persons ask if it is right to use Divine Power for personal purposes. No one thinks it wrong to use other laws of nature for personal purposes. The laws of Mind and Spirit are natural laws. The only difference between the use of them and other natural laws is that most people have not realized that they can use spiritual law as consciously as they do other laws.

Do not hesitate to use this law for any purpose which is constructive. It is no more selfish to use spiritual law for personal purposes than it is to plant a garden for your personal use. Moreover, there is no escaping this law, for it is as intimate as your own thought, as personal as your own being.

The world starves in the midst of plenty, weeps in the midst of joy. Yet the Eternal Manna has never ceased to fall. The fields of God are ripe unto harvest. The garden of your mind was planted by a Wisdom superior to yours. Enter in and possess this promised land. When you accept in simple faith, you will receive. When you knock in childlike belief, the door will be opened. What you seek with enthusiastic acceptance, you will find.

It makes little difference what method you use, provided you have conviction. Some will tell you that you should affirm the Divine Presence, denying all else. Well and good. This method will work. Others may tell you that all you need do is to ask, believing. They are right. Each receives according to his belief. Don't be too concerned over methods.

Any method that leads to conviction will produce results.

Stop arguing. Learn to believe. Stop debating. Learn to accept. Stop looking for an authority outside your own conviction. This calls for complete confidence in the Law and an equal confidence in yourself. If you wish to be healed you must expect to be made whole. If you wish freedom you must no longer think bondage. Bondage and freedom are but two ways of using one law. If you spend all your time saying, "I am poor, weak, sick, miserable and unhappy," you will attract poverty, weakness, sickness and unhappiness.

Use your intellect, imagination and feeling for the purpose of seeing and sensing freedom instead of bondage, joy instead of unhappiness, plenty instead of want, health in place of disease. The very denial of your good keeps that good from you. Reversing this process, through affirmation, will bring about the good you desire.

Open the gates of your consciousness to the Divine Presence and you will be flooded with light. Consciously commune with the Spirit and you will receive a direct answer. This answer will always fit your individuality because you are Life individualized.

No one can take your place. There is neither competition nor monopoly in Spirit. Coming daily to the Supreme Source of Being for inspiration and guidance, you will receive a new influx of Life, always fitted to your need. Communing with the Spirit you receive inspiration, you acquire confidence and faith, you rest in peace, you are poised.

From this spiritual consciousness your word becomes the law unto that thing whereunto it is spoken. It is acted upon by the Law of Life. Your authority is not one of egotism or arrogance. It is the authority which comes when one's consciousness is in tune with the Infinite.

Practice the Presence of the Spirit until your whole being is flooded with Its light. Say:

It is a law of my life that wherever I go the way shall be prepared before me, made immediate, perfect, plain, straight and easy.

I am compelled to see and understand every opportunity that presents itself, to operate upon it intelligently.

I am compelled to take any physical action necessary to the manifestation of this word.

The prayer of power is an affirmation so completely believed in that there is no longer any conscious or subconscious denial of it. When your prayer or treatment arrives at a complete acceptance, it will be answered. Enter the closet of your mind, close the door, speak with complete authority. You are one with an Infinite Presence which can inspire, one with a Universal Law which can execute. Say:

There is nothing in me that hinders the Spirit from manifesting Itself through me in joy, happiness and peace.

It is the law of my life that wherever I go I shall meet with joy, with love, friendship, gratitude, compensation—with a complete opportunity for the expression of every talent and ability I possess. Every door is open.

Nothing can go forth from me but goodness, truth, love, kindness; therefore, nothing less than goodness can come back to me.

When ideas of evil, lack or fear present themselves, exercise your dominion over them. Realize that your faith is the law of elimination to evil. There is no spiritual law of discord, sickness or lack. The laws of Spirit are complete, perfect and good. From the standpoint of the Life within you, anything that denies this is false.

You do not put power into your word; you take it out. When your word is based on Divine Love, Infinite Goodness and Eternal Peace, you may know that it is no longer the word of an isolated individual, it is the word of the Supreme Power in you—not some mighty, but Almighty. Say:

I identify myself with abundance, health and happiness.

I associate myself with the vast All.

I identify myself with everything necessary to make my life complete.

There is no depression, no fear, no sense of lack, insecurity or unworthiness.

I believe that God is All-in-All, over all, in everything that I shall ever meet.

I am filled with peace and confidence.

You are, as Emerson implied, an organ through which the Spirit executes Its will and performs Its act of creation. God does not depend on you. You do depend on God. Electrical energy exists independently of the appliance through which it operates. However, the mechanical device depends upon the electrical energy. It is only as this mechanical device permits a flow of energy that it can distribute it. So it is with your mind. Divine Energy flows through your thought.

The nature of the Mind Principle you are using is that wherever a mental image is set up in it, an objective form will be created. Learn to convert thought patterns of sickness, unhappiness, fear and doubt into patterns which conform to spiritual perfection. You cannot change a pattern of fear by maintaining an attitude of fear or by fluctuating between fear and faith. Make a picture of yourself as happy and successful. Refuse to entertain contrary ideas. Since you are the only one who has complete access to your thought, you can do this for yourself better than anyone else can do it for you.

You cannot be responsible for the acceptance of others. Each is an individual. Though you poured an ocean of love over one, he must receive it. A bucket that is turned upside down, even in a cloudburst, will not be filled. Though manna fall from heaven, one remains famished unless he eat.

It is not always easy for one to control his thoughts. It is not easy in the midst of pain to think peace, in the midst of poverty to think abundance, in the midst of unhappiness to think joy. But if you do this you will meet with success. The Law of Mind reflects your mental attitudes exactly as they are. Say:

That which I seek is seeking me.

That which belongs to me will come to me.

Since it is my desire that only good, truth, love, wisdom and power shall go from me, I know this is all that can come back to me.

The Kingdom of God is within and around me.

I know that the power of the living Spirit exists at the center of my being.

Now, think of some desire, and say:

It is done unto me.

Even God must wait your conscious cooperation before the full light of His presence and the power of His law can be made manifest through you. Your conscious co-operation with Him starts with a realization of the Divine Presence and your union with It. Say:

I know that the Presence, the Power and the Activity of the Living Spirit are in and around me.

Chapter VI

I know that the Law of God, which is perfect, is operating through me. I know that there is One Mind, that Mind is God, that Mind is my mind. There is no fear in this Mind, no memory of fear, no expectation of fear. There is no thought of want, of lack or limitation in this Mind. This Mind is functioning in me now.

Now make known your desires and accept them as manifest facts in your life. Every organ, function, action and reaction of your physical being, circulation, assimilation and elimination, are parts of a Divine Pattern which is forever perfect within you. Say:

There is no obstruction to the operation of this pattern.

There is no irritation, agitation or inflammation.

There is no sense of unhappiness or morbidity.

There is no confusion in Spirit.

Therefore, there is no confusion in my mind.

There is one divine circulation flowing through me which is never inhibited, retarded or congested.

This circulation is free, complete and perfect, automatically eliminating anything that does not belong to pure Spirit.

When you think with complete conviction, the Law of Mind will operate on your thought exactly as you think it, for the thing, condition or person you are thinking about. The repeated experience of thousands during the last fifty years has proved this. The principle you are using has been scientifically demonstrated. It is now merely a question of how effectively you use it. Say:

The Mind within me, being God, is not afraid of anything. It does not remember any unhappy experience, nor does it anticipate any. At the center of my being there is complete poise, perfect faith and confidence.

I am forever one with Spirit, in It and of It. I am an individualization of pure Spirit. There is no condemnation, no judgment, no sense of sin, sinner, mistake, punishment, burden, doubt or fear in me—no bitterness, no hate, no strife.

Chapter VII

YOUR FAITH can penetrate clouds of unbelief and reveal the Truth which is forever perfect. Your words do not create this Truth, they merely reveal It. By way of illustration, imagine yourself looking at the picture of a beautiful landscape. In this picture there are trees, a house, a stream of water, a beautiful meadow, and in the background mountains and a blue sky, dotted with clouds. You look at it long, contemplating its beauty.

Now, suppose that a colored glass is placed between you and the picture so that the picture appears blurred. Everything seems distorted and yet nothing has happened to the picture. It is your business to remove the colored glass. Because the picture is still there on the wall, it still may be seen.

Mental statements are merely a method you use for the clearing up of mental images. Neither affirmations, denials nor statements create the pattern of perfection, nor can they change it. They merely rearrange your thinking. If you could rearrange your thinking instantly, you would have an instantaneous result. If it takes time, do not become discouraged for you are working with a definite Principle which cannot fail you.

Your desire for self-expression is inherent in the Divine Pattern itself, and it is because you intuitively feel this Pattern that you grope back toward it. Learn to trust the intuition within you, which causes you to sense the Pattern. Say:

There is nothing in me which can obstruct the Divine Pattern.

I know that every organ, action and function of my being is acting in accord with the law of universal harmony.

All doubt, fear, confusion or uncertainty, is cast out of my mind.

There is a stream of Life running into every organ and function of your being. This stream is always there. It never stops for a second. If it did, the universe would cease to exist. Inexhaustible energy exists at the center of your being. Therefore, learn to live without effort. Activity is the joy of life flowing through you.

Since no two persons are alike there must be a unique place for you in the scheme of things. The Divine Pattern would be imperfect without you. Dare to be yourself. Stand in wonder before the majesty and might, the beauty and power of that Divine Presence which seeks expression through your individual life. Accept all the good there is. Whatever things you desire, believe that you have them. Say:

I surrender all fear, all doubt. I let go of all uncertainty I know there is no confusion, no lack of confidence.

I know that what is mine will claim me, know me, rush to me.

I accept the gift of Life for myself and for everyone else.

There should be a definiteness in your mental attitude, but no sense of coercion. There should be a one-pointedness without any attempt at concentration, a definite direction without trying to force anything. There should be a positive decision without compulsion.

If there is any doubt in your mind as to whether or not God or Life wishes you to have the best, ask yourself: Could God, who is freedom, conceive restriction? Could God, who is limitless, conceive lack, want, limitation or bondage? Could God, who is perfect life, conceive anything that limits the joy of living?

If God wills death, then God is not Life. If God wills lack, then God is limited. If God's will operates against peace, then God is confused. Nothing rewards or punishes you but the immutable law of cause and effect. There is no good which you cannot experience provided you first embody that good. There is no joy which you cannot reach provided you first clear your consciousness of anything which would limit this joy in yourself or in others. Expect, accept, and you shall receive. Say:

There is no judgment, no condemnation, no criticism.

I know that any belief in a power that damns, or a hell that waits, or any devil, is false.

Every such belief is eradicated.

Any effect of any such belief is wiped out.

There is no damnation, no judgment coming in or passing through me.

There is justice, knowledge, right government, divine guidance without judgment.

This does not mean that I accept lies or think that mistakes are as good as right action; it merely means that Divine Intelligence operates through me without confusion, calmly, forward moving, progressive, upward spiraling, outward reaching.

I am guided by Infinite Wisdom into that Light which is eternal.

My soul is jubilant.

The Will of God for you is the will of a boundless life, flowing through you. It is the will of joy, of success, of happiness, of peace, of abundance. It is the will of the Kingdom of Heaven, not absent from this earth, but imperfectly seen.

You cannot build happiness or sanity on the proposition that God wills evil, that there is a devil, a hell or a future punishment. The Law of cause and effect works at all times as absolute justice. While you would harm others you can be hurt yourself. While you withhold good you can have an equal amount of good withheld from you.

The ceaseless human struggle for liberty is an attempt to rise above the limitations which the consciousness of man knows to be false. Every scientific discovery is proof that limitation is not ordained by the laws of your being.

The Divine is always present and appears wherever recognized. As you enter more completely into conscious union with Life, you will realize that the universe holds as much good for you as you can take, that you can take only what you give.

You cannot draw love into your consciousness through hate. You cannot draw peace from confusion. You cannot see beauty through ugliness, nor hear harmony while your ears are filled with discord. Say:

God is right where I am.

God is what I am.

All that God has is mine now.

I enter into the conscious possession of this Divine Allness, this universal Bounty, this perfect Reality, today.

I know that it is manifesting in my life.

You rob no person when you discover your own good. You limit no person when you express a greater degree of livingness. You harm no one by being happy. You steal from no one by being prosperous. You hinder no person's evolution when you consciously enter into the kingdom of your good and possess it today.

Your thought, operating through the Law of Life, can meet your need, convert fear into faith, loss into gain, failure into success. Act as though you already had dominion over evil. Refuse to entertain images of fear. Know that good is the only power there is.

Believe that you are governed by Divine Intelligence, that you are directed by Divine Guidance. Know that everything you say, think or do that is constructive, is done through Divine Authority. Know that the freedom which already exists in the Mind of God belongs to you and now manifests through you. Say:

The Freedom of God is my freedom.

Chapter VII

The Power of God is my power.
The Presence of God is with me. The Mind of God is my mind.
The Strength of God is my strength. The Joy of God is my joy.
The consciousness that God is in and through everything will enable you better to see perfection and harmony in people and affairs. Know that the Spirit is right where you are. It is the very essence of your being. It is at the center as well as at the circumference of your life. Learn to sense this Divine Presence in every thought and act.
Let the warmth and color of this Presence permeate your entire consciousness. Let your thought be filled with an atmosphere of helpfulness, of life, of givingness and of peace. Know that the doorway of opportunity is never closed. Know that experience opens up before you like a blossoming flower. Live in continuous, joyous anticipation. Say:
The Spirit within me is God.
The Living Spirit Almighty is within me now.
Spirit is the sustaining Principle of my life.
I open my mind to Its influx.
I open my consciousness to Its inflowing.
It might come as a surprise to many if, when they say; "My poor head!" "My poor back!" or "My poor circulation!" you were to tell them they are actually using a creative law in a negative way. The laws of mind do not work in one instance while refusing to operate in another. Every time you think, you are using the Law of Mind. How careful, then, you should be to think constructively.
Mental laws are as real as physical laws, reproducing physical laws in the mental realm. The use of your creative power is as natural as the use of electricity, but there is not as much known about it. Many think it is something delivered only to a few by special edict. Fortunately, this is not the case.
When the Spirit thinks, knows or wills, a law is set in motion which projects and governs what It thinks, knows and wills. Since God is always in harmony with Himself and knows only that which is good, then God thinks only that which is good. Since God thinks everything into being, there must be a perfect pattern at the center of everything.
Your individual world is a unique and individualized representation of the whole universe, following the same laws, governed by the same principle, and stimulated by the same mind. Say:
The Mind of God is manifesting in my life.

Chapter VII

The Spirit within me is projecting Itself into my experience.
Divine Intelligence is acting in my affairs.
Everything that I do, say or think is governed by this Intelligence.
The Power which creates and sustains everything is now creating everything necessary to my happiness.
It is because the Law of Life is at the center of your being that your thought is creative. The Law of God acting through you makes your thought creative. It takes the form of your thought and reacts to your word exactly as you think it.
Your individual use of this Law becomes the law of your individual being. While this is one of the most profound concepts ever believed in, it is also one of the most simple. Instead of having an individual creative mind, you really have an individual or personal use of a Law which is infinite. Through this Law you can bring things to you from the uttermost parts of the earth.
The Mind Principle around you is reactive to your thought. Its chief characteristic is Its susceptibility to impression. It receives the slightest vibration of thought and acts upon it.

Since this Law acts like a mirror, when you withdraw old images of thought and place new ones in front of this mirror of Mind, the old reflections or conditions cease to exist and the new ones take their places. But if you only half withdraw the old images and only half create new ones, your experience will partake of the nature of both kinds of thought. Say:

I am not concerned about what happened yesterday.
I know that today everything is made new.
I let go of all sense of limitation.
I divorce my thought from any belief in lack.
I repudiate the idea that I am poor, weak, sick or unhappy.
New conditions are being created for me—conditions of harmony, happiness, peace and joy.
All circumstances and situations are being harmonized.
Wherever I go I shall meet peace, joy and happiness.
Whatever I do shall be done with reason and intelligence.
I shall be surrounded by friendship, by beauty, by right action.
My whole being responds to this conviction.
Simply, with complete conviction, I accept my freedom.

Chapter VIII

EVERYTHING YOU have ever thought, said, done, seen, learned or experienced, has left an imprint upon your subconscious mind. This subconscious also contains memory images of your family life, your ancestral background and the sum total of what the whole world has thought or believed.

These memories are not dead things. Quite the reverse, they are always active. But there is more to it than this. Just as you are being acted upon by your own memories, the mind of history and your environment, you are also being acted upon by the Mind of God which is within and around you.

Between this Divine Presence, this upper part of your being, and your outward experience, there is a field of subconscious reactions which have been gathered up throughout the ages. But you are a creator and not a creature. Today you may be suffering from the effects of the race consciousness and your own beliefs, but today you can begin to change them. Say:

I know that I am one with God.

I know that God in me is perfect.

I know that my real nature is spiritual.

I know that I exist in a boundless good, in a heavenly state, and in perfect being.

I know that my mind is being acted upon by pure Spirit.

Divine Intelligence guides me into peace, happiness and success, into joy, love and perfect life.

The desire you have to be something, to do something, is a mental echo in your mind of the Spirit which already exists within you. It is an impact of your divine and spiritual self upon your mental or psychological self. It is the Spirit in you seeking an avenue of expression through you. It is the real Self you would like to be, the deep spiritual Self having all knowledge, having access to all power, being one with Life. This is the Self that can heal the sick and raise the dead. It is a transcendent, triumphant self.

While it is true that suffering exists in the world, that poverty and unhappiness have been the common experience of mankind, it would be an unwise person who would ascribe these negations to the Divine Will. Those who would deny you the privilege of having the things you so earnestly desire in this world, hope themselves to receive them in the next life.

You are assuming that you are an immortal being now. You are assuming that the good which exists in the future, already exists in the present. Therefore, to place your good in the future is merely to delay your entering into the kingdom of heaven now. You are selfish only if you would affirm a good for yourself which you would withhold from others.

It simmers down to the word "goodness", to the concept of "kindness"—to the one Presence, which is Love, and to the one Principle, which is Law; to the one Person, which is God, and to yourself as a manifestation of this Divine Presence. Say:

Today I enter into my kingdom of joy, into my inheritance of happiness.

I know that every good purpose which I entertain is already accomplished.

I know that every constructive demand or request I make upon the universe is already granted.

I know that I am governed by Divine Law.

I know that I am inspired by Divine Intelligence and guided by Divine Reason.

If you wish to be successful you must identify yourself with success. The law of identity is a definite thing. That with which you mentally identify yourself sets up an image of thought in your consciousness which tends to attract the situations with which you are mentally identified. The subjective state of your consciousness, which means the sum total of your unconscious thought processes, is continually attracting or repelling. This process goes on beneath the threshold of the conscious mind.

People are often attracting things to themselves which they do not consciously desire, but with which they have become unconsciously identified. Say:

I expect everything I do to prosper.

I enthusiastically expect success.

I let good flow into my experience.

I am seeing good in every direction I look.

I am looking forward to more good.

I am entering into a deeper understanding of life.

I am recognizing my union with all people and all events.

The subjective state of your thought is an accumulation. While these subjective images of thought act as a cause as long as they are permitted to remain, they can be uprooted and others put in their place. It may take time to do this, but the reward is worth the effort. Your whole aim is to bring your

mind to a place where it unconsciously accepts the good it desires. Say:
I carefully guard my thought.
I refuse to permit anything antagonistic or unlovely to enter my
consciousness.

I am learning to live in joy, in peace and in calm confidence. I am putting my
whole trust, faith and confidence in the good. I think with clarity, move with
ease, and accomplish without strain.
Divine Guidance is yours for the asking. The answer to any problem which
can ever confront you already exists at the center of your being. It is not
enough merely to know that Divine Guidance exists—you must use it. You
use it by consciously recognizing its source within yourself and by
deliberately calling upon it, expecting it to answer.

In order that you may not receive false impressions, you can test the thoughts
that come to you. For instance, if you receive subconscious impressions
having the slightest element of destructiveness in them, you may know that
they do not emanate from a Divine source. For Life is not the author of
confusion, but of peace.
If you wish to be certain that the impressions that come to you are from the
Spirit, analyze them and see if they are of the nature of the goodness and
peace which the Spirit must be. God never sets one man's opinion against that
of another. God, being love, never wills hate or destruction. God, being
peace, never ordains confusion.
When a problem confronts you, take it into the silence of your consciousness.
Instead of thinking of the problem, think of the answer. God does not have
problems; therefore, the Divine Mind is the answer to every human problem.
Principles never have problems. Problems are solved by bringing them under
the control of principles. The problem is dissolved as the principle flows
through it to the correct answer.
Mentally act and think as though the problem were only an argument trying
to convince you that you do not know the answer. It is your business to
neutralize this argument, taking it apart, thought by thought, until there is
nothing left of it, until you reach a realization that dissipates it.
The Divine Presence will guide, guard and protect you. It will counsel you
with wisdom. Its might and majesty will enter into your being. It will sustain
and uphold you in everything you do. You will learn to talk with It and you
will receive direct intuitive answers. Faith is the essence of this communion.

Having recognized the Divine Presence as your guiding star of hope, assurance and certainty, be equally certain that you recognize the Universal Law of Mind as your servant. This Law is the Principle you are to use. Your faith in this Law causes It to act upon that faith, to bring into your experience those things you accept. All you need be sure of is that you never use this Law for destructive purposes. When you have complied with Love you can use the Law without any sense of limitation or fear. Say:

Letting go of all previous mistakes, I know that today I am free and unhindered.

I feel the operation of Divine Love and Universal Law in my affairs.

I know that everything I am doing is governed by Love and controlled through Law.

I am conscious that I am one with all people in love, in essence, and in joy.

It is certain that you cannot believe in abundance while identifying yourself with lack. Forget the lack and think only of abundance. Control your mental reactions so that they automatically become affirmative. This will be an interesting and happy experience, for you will be working in the laboratory of mind with the great Law of being. Abundance belongs to you. Good will come to you if you affirm its presence.

Learn how to think abundantly. Think of the vastness of everything, the limitlessness of space, the numberless grains of sand on the seashore—how abundant, how lavish nature is! Learn to see abundance in everything, to multiply the good you already possess. Be consciously one with the law of abundance. Expectancy will speed your progress. Say:

I believe the Law of Good will bring every good and perfect thing to me and will bless everyone I contact.

Now think of the thing you desire, and say:

I know that the Law of Good is operating upon this idea.

I speak this word with implicit confidence, belief and acceptance.

I know that it shall not return unto me void.

I know that I shall experience the good which 1 now affirm.

Your subconscious mind is the medium between unconditioned good and the amount of that good you shall experience. The operation of your subconscious mind is that of a silent force within you which holds up its images of thought to the Universal Law of Mind which, in Its turn, reflects into your experience the things you inwardly believe.

Your problem is to change these subjective images of thought, so that you will automatically attract good. There are no exact formulas for doing this. You will do well to work out your own method, always remembering that definite statements produce definite results when these statements are sincerely believed in. For example, you might use the following thoughts. Say:

I know that I am drawing my good to me.

There is a silent power of attraction within me which is irresistible.

Now mention to yourself something which you wish to bring into your experience. Think it over for a moment so that you have a clear idea of it, and say:

I know that everything in my experience is working together to bring this about.

I am filled with calm confidence, with expectancy of good.

I know that this particular thing is transpiring in the invisible at this very moment, and that it will become a part of my visible experience.

Everything within me accepts this.

Expectancy speeds progress; therefore, live in a continual state of expectancy. No matter how much good you are experiencing today, expect greater good tomorrow. Expect to meet new friends. Expect to meet new and wonderful experiences. Try this magic of expectancy and you will soon discover a dramatic side to your work which gives full vent to constructive feeling. It makes life a game that is a joy to play. It enables you to enter into the spirit of things and of people. Say:

Today, and every day, I expect good.

I anticipate meeting new friends.

I joyously anticipate contacting new situations which will increase my livingness.

My life is an adventure.

I know that wonderful things are going to happen to me.

I know that everything I do shall turn into good for myself and for others.

You have a right to know that when you live in harmony with the Divine Presence around you, you will be protected by Its omnipotent power. No harm can come to you when you know that God is at the center of everything. This knowledge will protect you from all evil. Evil is as night before the on-rushing light of your consciousness. It is as darkness dissipated by the sun of your faith. It is as fire extinguished by the waters of your spirit.

Your enthusiastic anticipation and happy contentment water the seed of faith which you have placed in the soil of Divine Substance. Believing this, do not delay the joy of possessing until tomorrow. There are no tomorrows in the Divine Mind. Your tomorrow is merely more of God's today.

Back of every event, the slightest effort you make, the smallest concept you entertain, there is an inexhaustible reservoir of life, of imagination, energy and will, flowing through you into action. Keep it as simple as this, and think about it until it becomes as natural to you as walking and talking.

Divine Power exists everywhere and takes form for you through your ideas, your faith. You neither create this energy nor hold it in place. All that your faith does is to form a mold through which it may take a temporary form.

Place a mirror in front of you, hold before it what you call a small object, such as a pencil, and you will see that the reflection is neither larger nor smaller than its image. Now remove the pencil and place a book in front of the mirror. Instantly the mirror reflects the larger object. Suppose you had a mirror large enough for you to place a mountain in front of it. Would not the mirror as easily reflect the image of the mountain? It would not be hard. It would not be easy. It would not be large. It would not be small. It would merely be a reflection.

Life is a mirror reflecting your images of thought. If you see confusion in this mirror, don't blame the law of reflection, don't even bother to blame yourself, but be willing to acknowledge that this confusion must be a reflection of your own consciousness.

"But," you may say, "it is really a reflection of the confusion around me." Maybe so, but unless this confusion around you had found entrance to your consciousness it could not be reflected in your mirror. No doubt many of the reflections are caused by the images of thought entertained through previous years of disappointment, uncertainty and doubt. But this must not discourage you.

Learn to sit at home with the cause, to reaffirm your position in life, to remold your consciousness, and you will see that the reflections will change. Just as a gardener pulls up old plants that are no longer desirable, so you will uproot the images of thought which you no longer wish to experience. You will plant new thoughts in the garden of your mind, and you will reap a new harvest. Say:

I know that I can make conscious use of the Divine Law of my being.

I know that this Law reacts immediately and creatively to my faith.

I know that when I speak this word for myself, there is a direct reaction toward me.

I know that when I speak it for others, there is a direct reaction toward them.

Chapter VIII

There is no doubt or uncertainty in my consciousness.
I identify myself with the good I desire.
I have complete confidence that the Law of Good will respond to me by creating the object of this desire.
I have a quiet contentment and an inner sense of peace.
I have an enthusiastic sense of well-being. I know that all the power there is, is for me; therefore, I put on the whole armor of faith. I am free Spirit, I am perfect Life. I am in conscious union with the God who is right where I am.

Chapter IX

IF YOU wish to know the truth about your business or your profession, know that it is an activity of good. It is an activity of your partnership with the Infinite. The business of life is to be happy, active and whole, to express the Divine Life with joy and in fulfillment.

Lift the load of personal responsibility by transferring it to the Law of perfect action. No matter what confronts you, what obstructions appear or what undesirable situations exist in your experience, this Law can dissolve them.

This Law knows neither big nor little. It is like nature's law of gravitation which holds a feather to the surface of the earth and also holds the mountain steadfast. It does not say, "Behold, I am strong in one place and weak in another." It does not ask you to weigh the mountain or the feather. Throw a small pebble over a cliff and at the same time roll a giant boulder into space —each will find its way to earth. The law of gravitation works automatically on big and little.

So it is with your problems. Don't think some of them are hard and others easy. Shift the load of those which appear weighted, as well as those which appear light, into the Law of action. Big and little are swallowed up in one comprehensive whole. Who can say that the blossoming of a rose in the desert is of less importance to the Divine Imagination than the building of an empire?

You exist that Divine feeling, fire, imagination and creativity may be expressed through you. The Spirit comes to you with a new and fresh creativity. You need not ask what others have done or how they have done it. Be yourself and express life as you find it. Never imitate. Trust the self. Find the self in God and God in the self.

Thought has a cumulative power. If you daily say to yourself that your word uproots and casts out every thought of fear or uncertainty, it will surely do so. When thoughts of fear or discouragement assail you, turn to them quietly and say:

You have no place in me.

There is nothing in me that can entertain thoughts of negation or doubt.

I refuse to admit them.

I know that my word casts out fear and doubt.

It converts fear into faith.

I know there is nothing in the universe that wishes me ill.

There are no negative forces operating in, around, or through me.

There is but One Mind, which is my mind.

This true Mind within me has never received an image of doubt.

The God Mind within me entertains only that which is perfect.

There is a pattern of perfection at the center of your being which has never been touched by disease or misfortune. Your intellect senses this through intuition; your imagination feels it by divine right; your inward consciousness knows it through faith. What you are trying to do is to awaken your whole being to spiritual awareness.

It is the intellect and the subconscious self which need renewing. The Spirit neither sleeps nor slumbers. The Spirit is God. Any maladjustments in your life will be healed when you realize this perfect center within yourself. The vision you must catch and hold is the consciousness of a union so complete and perfect that you find no difference between your own being and God. The two are one.

What thought has planted, thought can uproot. The conditions laid down by mental attitudes, whether or not you are conscious of them, can be changed. If you are experiencing some condition which is unhappy, you must know there is nothing in you that attracts this condition, nothing in you that holds it in place, nothing in you that believes it must be this way. Turn your mind entirely from the condition and think in an exactly opposite manner. Say:

There is nothing in me that can entertain doubt.

There is no fear, discouragement or uncertainty.

I am filled with confidence, with the expectancy of good, with the knowledge that the Spirit is always triumphant.

I know that my word definitely reverses any and every negative situation.

In actual practice, you reverse the old thought patterns by definitely knowing that they can no longer operate through you. This is more than a theory. Thoughts of peace will reverse thoughts of confusion. A consciousness of faith will reverse fear. It is now known that fear and discouragement, the feeling of unworthiness and inferiority, as well as a sense of uncertainty about one's relationship to God, probably start with an unconscious sense of rejection. Out of this comes the sense of uncertainty, fear of the future, the anxiety complex, the insecurity attitude, the feeling of not being wanted, the sense of guilt.

These thought patterns are more or less laid down in every man's life. Your business is not to bother about where they came from but to know how to get rid of them. If you have a sense of uncertainty, of inferiority, of rejection, say:

The Spirit never rejects me.
I accept myself.
I realize my center in the Divine Mind.
I know that I am one with all the good there is.
I am one with all the power there is.
I am one with all the peace there is.
I know there is nothing in me that can condemn or be condemned.
There is nothing in me that can judge or be judged.
I know that my word uproots any sense of rejection from my consciousness.

The Spirit is neither sad nor depressed. If you would catch the vision of the joy which should be yours, you must dry your tears, you must lay aside your fears, you must think from the inspirational center within you which is nothing less than the Divine in you singing Its song of life.

The wick of your individual life runs deep into the oil of pure Being. There is but One Life and that Life is your life now. No matter what confusion appears at the surface of your life, there is always a place of calm at the center of your being. No matter how turbulent the waves may be on the ocean of your experience, beneath there is a changeless peace. Your being is submerged but not lost in the Infinite.

When you become confused, stop and listen to your inner calm. Turn from the confusion to that deeper something within. Say:

I am submerged in peace.
I am surrounded by peace.
I am immersed in peace.
There is nothing but peace.
Peace—deep, calm, undisturbed.

You will find that the confusion disappears. The light which the storm seemed to have extinguished again becomes steady. Peace comes from a sense of union with the whole. Confusion comes from a sense of separation. Confusion comes because you are looking only at the surface. If you put a straight stick in a pool of water and then ruffle the surface of the pool, the stick will appear bent. It is not bent, however; it is merely a disturbance at the surface of the water that causes it to appear bent. If you swim under water beneath the disturbed surface and open your eyes, you will see a straight stick. The bent stick really was an illusion.

So it is with confusion. It exists as a condition but not as a reality. The mirage is in your own consciousness. If confusion comes, take your intellect and dive deep into your pool of peace. Through an act of faith open your eyes and you will see that there is no confusion.

Rising above confusion, you affirm the Divine Presence in all Its beauty, power and peace. From this fundamental affirmation your consciousness becomes imbued with a sense of power as well as of peace. You are now in a position to turn to any specific condition of discord, and, speaking with complete authority, to know that your word will reverse it Say:

The Spirit within me makes all things new.
Every negative thought or condition is erased from my experience.
I am aware of my union with Good.
I am conscious of my oneness with Life.
I expect more prosperity, more happiness, more harmony than ever before.
I walk in the joy of ever-increasing good.

Get it firmly fixed in your consciousness that just as there are laws of physics, there are spiritual and mental laws which act in an identical manner. Have confidence in the laws of Mind and Spirit, and in your ability to use them. Think of them as naturally as you do of other laws of nature. Say:

I know that I am living in a universe of law and order, in a universe of pure Spirit, of Divine Intelligence.
I know that I am surrounded by and immersed in the Mind of God.
The Mind of God is flowing through me.
I live, move and have my being in pure Spirit.
The Mind of God is right where I am.

It is ever available and always operating.

Your meditation consciously used for definite purposes is a spiritual mind treatment. Your spiritual realization automatically acts upon the Law of Mind which is around you and in you. You will recognize this as the secret of the prayer of faith throughout the ages. It is the secret of the effectiveness of all modern metaphysical movements, no matter what they call themselves. There is no one-and-only way to understand or use the Law of Mind.

Chapter IX

Realize that the Divine Presence is ever with you, that there is no place where you leave off and God begins. Here, in quiet confidence and calm peace, make known your desires. They are not prayers in the sense of petition. They are, rather, what Emerson called the thoughts of "a jubilant and a beholding soul."

When working for yourself say, "I am." When working for someone else say, "He is," or "She is." When you say "I am," you are directing your treatment to yourself. When you say, "He is," or "She is," you are directing it for someone else.

Your affirmation (prayer of faith or treatment) will reach a level in your experience, or in the experience of those whom you wish to help, equal to the level of realization in your own consciousness when you make your affirmation. It is like water reaching its own level by its own weight. Say:

I know that I live under the government of Divine Law.

I know that I live in the presence of Divine Love.

I surrender everything that seems imperfect to that which is complete and whole.

There is no anxiety, no tension, no strain.

There is no doubt, no uncertainty.

I know that it is impossible for me to be separated from the Kingdom of God which is within and around me.

I live in this Kingdom here and now.

In this Kingdom there is peace, power and plenty.

Always feel that your treatment (your statement of truth) will meet any condition instantly, while, at the same time, being willing to work patiently until the condition is met. In each separate treatment (or statement of truth) believe that the work is already accomplished. Your treatment is really complete when your entire subjective reaction complies with, responds to, or embodies, the spirit and the meaning of the words you use. Persistence, flexibility and patience are necessary for the best results.

With a good-natured flexibility with yourself, learn to rise from confusion into peace, from sadness into joy. There is no law for you but your own soul shall set it, under the one great Law of all life. Turn to the Light within. Believe in yourself. Have confidence in the high impulsions that come to you. Listen deeply to the Divine Nature which forever more imparts Itself to you. Spirit is absolute, unlimited and ever available. Spirit is right where you are. Spirit fills all space, flows through all form, creates everything, governs everything through love, controls everything through law, expresses life and beauty in everything. Say:

There is one Power, one Presence and one Life.

The living Spirit is right where 1 am, within, around and through me.

I am in Spirit.

Spirit is in me.

Spirit knows in me.

Spirit sees through me, thinks in my mind, acts through my act.

This wellspring of Life, flowing up through me, knows no obstruction, no congestion, no imperfection.

There is a pattern of perfection at the center of my being, a divine and heavenly pattern of wholeness.

Every organ, action and function of my being is spiritual.

The Spirit is perfect in every part of my being.

I live in peace, in joy, and in perfect life.

Chapter X

IF YOU could become consciously and subjectively aware, even for one moment, of your true spiritual perfection, there would come such a conversion of your mind as instantly to heal your physical body. This is not the easiest thing to do. When you are in pain it is difficult to affirm peace. When you are in want it is hard to affirm abundance. But what you lose is a false sense of being. You are trading the unreal for the real, the false for the true.

If you wish to be happy, take all unhappiness out of your mind and bury it. If you want God, stop thinking about the devil. If you wish to live in the kingdom of heaven, forget hell.

You are to find the roots of your life in pure Spirit, to see the basic unity of all—the fundamental, mathematical and logical necessity of such a unity. Lose your sense of being separated from your good and you will find that you are united with it. This is the secret you have with the God who is ever with you. He already knows what you are trying to find out.

The next time any obstacle appears on your path, try to realize that it is not an entity, person or self-created condition. It is not true to the larger Life within you. Satisfy your mind that it is not a thing in itself. Cease fighting it and begin to realize its opposite. Know there are no obstructions in Spirit and that you already are Spirit. Begin to identify yourself with the Truth which knows no obstruction. Begin to claim your divine inheritance. Say:

I know there is no negation in God. I know that God is always right where I am.

I know that at the center of my being there is a positive affirmation of life.

My word erases anything within me that denies the presence of this Life.

There is One Life, that Life is God, that Life is my life now.

There is nothing in me that can deny the presence of this Life.

Everything within me affirms Its presence.

I have an inward sense and feeling of this Divine Presence at all times.

When everyone believed the world to be flat they did not flatten the round world. When one man made up his mind that the world was really round, he did not resist the flat world because he knew there was no such world. He set out to sail around the world he knew to be round. Through his act of faith he discovered the truth about the round world. The fear and superstition of others did not deter him. The accumulated experience of the race could not bind him. The belief that the unknown oceans were filled with monsters did not frighten him. He knew the world was round and that he could sail around it.

You have discovered the spiritual universe. Many others have discovered this same world, but each must make the discovery for himself. You are going to have a lot of joy sailing around this world of yours. Don't fight the opinions of others, or waste your time arguing over these things. Follow the inward gleam of your consciousness and you will arrive.

Whatever you identify yourself with you will become like. Whatever you resist until you make it a reality, you will also become like. Therefore, "... resist not evil and it will flee from you." Don't fight your fears; see through them. There is nothing in God's world to be afraid of. Say:

I know there is a spiritual center within me which is perfect.

I am now telling my own consciousness automatically to ward off any thoughts of doubt or uncertainty.

I sense that every state of doubt, every consciousness of negation is leaving me.

Every doubt is being converted into certainty.

Fear is being converted into faith.

I have an abiding sense of happiness and peace.

I am the very essence of peace.

1 have an inward confidence in my oneness with Good.

I rest in sublime trust.

There is only one God, one Divine Mind. This One is undivided, hence all of It is present everywhere.

God is not only where you are, He is what you are. In a sense, you might say, "Since God is all there is, the only Presence there is, and since the Spirit is manifest through everything, then everything I see is a manifestation of God. That within me which enables me to see, know and understand this, also is God. Since God does not go in search after Himself, I need no longer go in search after Him. Rather, I shall now live and think from the union which I already have." Say:

There is That within me which knows.

I am not only one with this Power, this Power is actually flowing through me now.

I am not only unified with the Divine Presence around me, this Presence is my presence.

It is the presence of my real and true self.

I am forever one with Life.

Chapter X

Your endeavor is not to locate the Divine Presence or awaken the activity of the Law. It is, rather, to become aware of this Presence and of Its activity flowing through you.

It will be well to consider the difference between outlining and choosing. As an individual, you have the right to choose. Being an individual, you cannot escape the necessity of choice. You are not an automaton. You are not a mental mechanism. You are not merely an aggregation of mental reactions. You are a person, a divine being in your own right. The Spirit has set the stamp of individuality upon Itself and called it you. What God has done you cannot undo. When you think, it is the Divine Mind in you willing Itself into action, thinking Itself into manifestation, realizing Itself as the object of Its own thought.

You do the choosing, the Law does the outlining. This is the distinction between choice and outline. If you choose to plant a tomato seed you have chosen a tomato plant, but you do not outline how many leaves shall grow on the plant, how many stalks it shall have. That belongs to the Law of cause and effect.

When you say, "I know that the Divine Intelligence is attracting certain conditions to me," and when you have affirmed your union with good, you can go about the business of everyday life with no sense of anxiety, knowing that the Law is working for you. The Law can only operate on your images of thought since the Law is a doer and not a knower. Therefore, it is up to you to keep these images clear that they may reflect themselves in the Law, which is a mirror. Say:

The Kingdom of God, the Glory of God, is here and now.

I am forever a part of Its being.

The perfect Law of God is now operating in my affairs.

There is no strain, stress or fear in my life.

I am in the presence of radiant Joy, of Divine Love and perfect Power.

You have been told that you should fast and pray. Perhaps true fasting is a determination no longer to entertain negative thoughts; perhaps it means continually to be affirming the good. The act of physical fasting is merely a symbol of this inward grace. The need for the symbol disappears when you understand its meaning. It is a good practice to fast, so far as the negative is concerned, and feast on affirmations only. Why not fast from the idea of lack and feast on the idea of abundance?

In no way does this mean that you need withdraw from the world and its activities. You should enter into these activities with a new sense of reality, with a penetrating spiritual vision which sees through the effect to its cause and knows this cause to be good.

It is certain that you must fast from fear if you wish to establish faith. You must fast from confusion if you hope to enter into tranquility. It matters not if your transition from the negative into the affirmative seems slow, if the ascent from your valley of negation to the mountaintop of realization seems difficult. Each step will bring you nearer the summit.

There is a Divine awareness within you which will lead you upward and onward. Prepare yourself for the ascent, then, filling your mental life with spiritual realization. Your bread is manna from heaven, your meat the living word, your fruit the inspiration of hope, your wine the essence of joy. Say:

I am aware of the Divine within me.

Peace, quiet and confidence flow through my thought.

I know that inspiration and guidance are mine.

I permit myself to be moved upon by Divine Intelligence.

Laying aside every sense of burden or false responsibility, losing all fear and uncertainty from my thought, I enter into my kingdom of good today.

I know that this kingdom is accessible to all.

You should always expect instantaneous and permanent results from your treatments. Unless you expect such results, you cannot attain them, since your denial of such results would be using the Law in reverse. Practice a complete abandonment to faith. This you must do for yourself. No one else can do it for you. If someone else could do this for you, you would not be you; you would be someone else. You cannot live outside yourself and no one can live for you. You alone can be yourself. Every great soul has known this. This is the greatest of all truths, the apex of all summits. Say:

I see through all physical and mental obstructions to the one perfect Presence within me.

I see through all apparent contradictions to the one perfect Being in every person.

I see through all confusion to the one Divine Presence at the center of everything.

When you say that your body is spiritual, you are not denying your physical body. The physical is included within, and is part of, the spiritual universe. You do not say, "I have no eyes, or feet, or stomach." They are part of the spiritual body.

God's world is not a world of illusion but of realities. Everything that is exists for the purpose of expressing Life. You are able to recognize the things around you because they are in the same Mind in which you live, the one Mind which is everywhere present. This means the Presence in everything— a tree, a rose, everything in nature, your own physical body. Nothing can be excluded from this omnipresence. It was this Presence that Moses communed with by the burning bush, the Divine Flame which surrounded the bush with an aura of light and color. This flame of Divinity penetrates everything.

If the Spirit has seen fit to express Itself through a physical universe and to give you a physical body, it would be absurd to think of this body or environment as an illusion unworthy of your attention. Rather, you should think of them as things of joy. Know that even the physical universe will respond to you when you respond to it. Say:

My body is a temple of the living Spirit. It is spiritual substance.

Every part of my body is in harmony with the living Spirit within me.

The life of this Divine Spirit flows through every atom of my being, revitalizing, reinvigorating and renewing every particle of my physical body.

There is a pattern of perfection at the center of my being which is now operating through every organ, function, action and reaction.

My body is a Divine Idea forever renewed by the Spirit.

Stop blaming anyone or anything—persons, circumstances or situations— for what may be happening to you. This is futile. It is a dead-end road. It is a blind alley. It is a raft adrift on an ocean of uncertainty. Today you are going to take your life in your own hands, realizing God is ever with you. You are going to identify yourself with goodness and with joy. Straight thinking is going to do this for you. Straight thinking may not be the easiest thing in the world, but it is possible for anyone. Say:

The Spirit within me is alive, awake and aware.

It is always flowing through me in perfect life.

I accept my spiritual perfection.

I know that my physical being is included in it.

It is a manifestation of the life, the energy, the love, the peace and the power which is of the Spirit.

I know that this day in which I live, this present time, which is now, is perfect. Everything in my world works harmoniously, divinely. I live in a

completeness of this present moment.
I know that the All-wisdom guides me, the All-power protects me, The All-presence goes with me.

Chapter XI

YOU USE the same power to drive your automobile forward, or, in reverse, to move it backward. The energy is not good when it moves you forward nor evil when it moves you backward. You must eliminate the idea of good and evil as entities opposing each other and realize that there is but one Life Principle. There is but one electric energy wherever it may be used, but one creative Spirit wherever It is perceived, but one spiritual Power wherever It is understood.

Like the ethers of space, the creative Principle of Life is ever present. Being everywhere present It must be present in you. Hence, It must be available at the center of your being.

That which defeats you when you use It in a limited way, gives you victory when you change your attitude toward It, permitting It to flow through you in a more extensive manner. Always It responds by corresponding to your mental attitudes. Say:

I now accept all that I have hoped for and believed in.

There is nothing in me that can doubt that good will make its appearance in my experience.

There is nothing in me that can dissipate my faith or dim its clear realization.

I see in everyone that which I know to be true about myself.

Therefore, everyone I think of is blessed by my thought.

You are never limited by the Principle of your being. Limitation is a result of a limited use of this Principle. You can come to but one conclusion: there is something which honors your belief, not in a big way in one place and in a little way in another; rather, it honors your belief as you believe it.

This Principle must be without limit. Your thought and acceptance can put brakes on it. In this way, paradoxical as it sounds, you limit the Limitless. Of course, you really do not limit It, but you do limit Its flow in your own experience.

Why is it that you do not instantly heal if the Principle with which you deal is limitless, unless it is that your use of this Principle is limited? Surely, it is within the province of the Divine easily to dissolve a cancer or a state of poverty. Surely, the miracle of faith can take place in your experience. Do you really expect the signs following your belief? You seem to when you pray, you feel you are using the right words, but are you sure that your prayers or affirmations are made with complete acceptance? It is not the form of the treatment which you give, or the prayer which you make, that gives it power. Rather, it is your faith. Say:

I know that I am in the Spirit of God.
I know that the Spirit of God is in me.
I know that this Spirit is complete and perfect.
Therefore, It must be complete and perfect in me.
I know that this Spirit is now operating in my affairs.
It is manifesting Its beauty and harmony in everything I do.
I know that my body is a spiritual idea, manifesting in form.
I know that every organ of my body, being a manifestation of pure Spirit, contains within itself a pattern of joy, of peace, of divine order, of harmony and complete perfection.

Suppose you wish to help a lonely person. Explain to him that God is present in everyone, that there is but One Person in Whom he lives, moves and has his being. Tell him that all people are in this One Person, that each is an individualized center of Spirit. He is already one with everyone else through the Spirit of all. Teach him how to see this One in all.

You can follow a very simple practice for him. This takes place in your own consciousness. Since it is difficult for him to identify himself with good, because he is immersed in a sense of isolation, spiritually you are going to take him by the hand until he learns to walk by himself.

Remember, a spiritual mind treatment is a series of statements for yourself or for someone you wish to help. You begin your treatment by realizing the Divine Presence which includes everything and everyone; by knowing that since God is over all, in all and through all, God is in this person. Say:

This word which I speak is for (naming the person).
He is one with God at this moment.
He is one with every person whom he meets.
There is no thought of separation or isolation in him.
Every thought which has denied his unity with people is dissolved.
He is inwardly conscious of his union with all people.
He thinks he is alone in the world. You know that he is one with all people. This unity of life is forever established. There is no real isolation, no real disunion, only an apparent one. His thought of loneliness and isolation holds people away from him. Clear this thought and the One in all people rushes out, in a sense, to meet Itself. You are working with an immutable Principle and when the thought is changed, the demonstration will be made. He will

find himself surrounded with friendship, love and appreciation.

That which is definite and clear in your own consciousness becomes a part of his consciousness and begins to work automatically for him. In the long run, he must learn to think for himself. You are merely helping him over a rough spot. You are doing this gladly, lovingly. He hopes that what you are thinking is true. He hopes for results. You expect them. He would like to believe. You must know. What he waits for, you accept. What he thinks may happen in the future, you know is happening right now. Your statements are always affirmations of the present, not the future.

Cultivating your own thought, living in continuous expectancy and affirmation, knowing the truth in season and out of season, you are doing your part. The Law will never fail you. Your problem is to convert your own thinking. You do this through words, audibly or inaudibly expressed; through thoughts, ideas, beliefs, prayer (which is silent communion with the Invisible), realization, meditation—whatever you choose to call the process.

Words are molds into which the creative substance of your consciousness flows. Words without meaning, while they may have some effect through constant repetition, cannot have the same effect that words with meaning have. Your words will have meaning in such degree as you actually feel that they are the activity of the Spirit within you.

Here is a fine point in using the Power within you. You must develop a spiritual awareness which is transcendent, which knows that it is as easy for the Truth to say, "Get up and walk," as it is for a tired -man to say, "Lie down and rest."

This calls for faith and understanding—a complete conviction that God is right where you are, that Life is speaking through you, and that the Law of Life is obeying your will. Words without this awareness have no power. Spiritual awareness is the healing agency loosed through your word. While it is true that thoughts are things, they are things in your experience only in such degree as your inward consciousness pours the fire of conviction into the form of your intellectual affirmation.

It is neither the Power, the Presence, nor the Law that you lack, if you do lack anything. It is a consciousness, an inner spiritual awareness. This consciousness is a thing of thought and conviction. It is a thing of faith and understanding. No one can give this to you but yourself, and if you have it no one can take it away from you. Say:

Truth lives forevermore at the center of my being.

Chapter XI

I know that faith is at the center of my own being.
I know that inner calm is accessible to me today.
I know that the Truth within me is always triumphant.
I   know   that   God   is   right   where   I   am.

When you give a spiritual mind treatment you are focusing a power and giving conscious direction to something which has accumulated within you through continual recognition. The peace your intellect affirms must be backed by a consciousness generated through perhaps repeated and laborious effort. The reward is worthy of the endeavor. If at all times you are seeking inwardly to be aware of the Divine Presence, you will find it easier and easier to direct the Law of Life for definite purposes. Say:

I know there is an inner Presence in everything.
I know that this Presence responds to me.

I recognize Spirit and It responds to me.
I realize that everything is alive, awake and aware with Spirit.

I commune with this Divine Presence.

The Spirit within me reaches out and communes with the Spirit in everything and everyone I contact.
It is the same Spirit in all, over all, and through all.

Chapter XII

GOD WITHIN you knows by pure intuition; that is, without process of reasoning with reference to external facts or existing conditions. If God were to know in any other way, He would be finite. This is why it is said that God is omniscient or all-knowing. Such omniscience or all-knowingness exists at the very center of your being. Therefore, Divine Guidance exists at the center of your being, acting as a principle in nature.

If you are living in an Intelligence which instantly knows the answer to any problem, then you are living in an Intelligence which has no problem. You are, therefore, bringing your problem to a Principle which has no problem, just as electricity, or mathematics, or the law of gravitation has no problem. Hold up an object heavier than the air and let go of it and the law of gravitation will bring it to the earth. It would be a problem if you had to force this object to the earth. It is no problem to the law, which works automatically. You let go of the object and the rest is automatic. So it is with the use of other principles in nature. So it is with Divine Guidance.

Common sense will tell you that Divine Guidance cannot exist for a few persons. It cannot exist because of any particular religious belief or because of a dogmatic acceptance of any creed. Divine Guidance must exist for you and for everyone, or not at all—just as electricity exists for everyone.

Divine Guidance, like the Presence of God, is where you are, at the center of your being. When you turn to the Spirit for the solution of your problem, Spirit answers by intuitively knowing, not the problem, but its answer. If you have a problem of confusion and wish to gain peace, this could not be done by asking God to be peace, for God is peace. Your answer would come as you turn from the confusion to the contemplation of peace. You cannot join confusion with peace. You must forget the one if you would unify with the other. Say:

Knowing that the Law of God is perfect, I lay aside all fear, uncertainty or doubt.

There is no burden whatsoever in my consciousness.

I live in the Kingdom of Heaven now.

I rejoice in the Divine Presence.

I bathe in the sunlight of eternal Truth.

I consciously enter into the benediction of Peace.

As your consciousness lifts itself above the problem into a spiritual atmosphere of affirmation, the problem, as such, disappears and the answer takes its place. Every problem contains its own answer if you think of the problem merely as a question, an inquiry, and not as an obstruction. Thinking of it this way, keep your mind not on the repetition of thoughts about the problem, but on the receipt of a definite answer.

Work with your consciousness until it ceases to function on the level of problem and begins to function on the level of answer. It is mathematically certain that your problem will be solved if you do this. You may not find this the easiest thing in the world to do, but even though it may be difficult at times, you must never permit yourself to become discouraged. The reward is certain.

Remember, you are not presenting God with the problem. God has no problem. Principles have no problems. God knows intuitively and the principle of Divine Guidance works automatically on your acceptance. Therefore, when you bring your hopes and aspirations to the Divine Center within you, lay them on the altar of your faith in complete confidence. Say:

The Spirit within me knows the answer to any problem which confronts me.

I now turn from the problem to the Spirit, accepting the answer.

I turn from any thought of confusion to a consciousness of peace.

I know that the Spirit of God is within me and the Law of God is around me.

I know that the answer (think of the problem, not as a problem, but merely as a question) is here and now.

It is within my own mind, because God is right where I am.

In calm confidence, in perfect trust, in abiding faith and with complete peace, I let go of the problem as a problem.

I receive the answer as fulfillment.

This is the secret of the answer to prayer. For, no matter what particular religious conviction the one praying may have, in the act of effective prayer he opens his consciousness to a Divine influx. That which is forever pressing against him flows through him, instructs his intellect, deepens his will, and executes its law through his act.

Through Divine intuition consciously enter the upper field of your mind where peace and joy forever exist. Do this humbly, but with a sense of triumph; meekly, but with a consciousness of worthiness—not timidly, as one knocking at a door which may refuse to open, but boldly, as one who knows in Whom he has believed.

You are working with an immutable Law, an unfailing Principle, an ever-available Power. It is as simple as this. The mind that is in you is the Mind of God. It knows nothing about big or little, hard or easy, but what It does for you It must do through you. Hence, you must believe before It can operate for your benefit. Say:

Realizing that the Divine Spirit can give me only what I receive, knowing that what the Spirit does for me It must do through me, I now accept the gift of Life.

I permit Infinite Life to flow through me.

I permit Divine Intelligence to act through me, knowing that all the power there is, all the presence there is, and all the life there is, is God, the Living Spirit Almighty.

Identify yourself with the object of your desire. Think of beauty and peace and you will attract peace and beauty. Watch yourself and see if you are believing that any condition or situation, past, present or future, can limit your use of this Divine Law. If you do, you are automatically causing the Law to work through that limiting condition. You are conditioning the Law to your own acceptance. This does not mean that you are limiting the Law. You are merely saying: This is what I expect of life. In other words, you are believing that the possibility of your personal experience is already set by your environment. Say:

The Law of good is flowing through me.

I am one with the rhythm of Life.

There is nothing to be afraid of.

There is nothing to be uncertain about.

God is over all, in all and through all.

God is right where I am.

I am at peace with myself.

I am at peace with everyone around me.

I am at peace with the world in which I live.

I am at home with the Divine Spirit in which I am immersed.

Let us think about happiness. Everyone desires to be happy. Everyone strives toward happiness. Too few obtain it. Happiness is not a mental debauch. If one must become intellectually or emotionally intoxicated to be happy, then, like one who has imbibed too much alcohol, he is bound sooner or later to sober up and must again plunge himself into an unnatural state to revive his happiness. Happiness must come from a deeper wellspring of being.

Permanent happiness comes from a quiet contentment and an inner sense of certainty which cannot be shaken by outside conditions, whether good or ill. The mind must reach a place where it no longer remembers the past with anxiety, or looks into the future with uncertainty. If you believe in Divine

Goodness, the loving-kindness and givingness of God, if you believe in your own soul as immortal, forever expanding, then no matter what situation confronts you, you can be happy. Say:

I have a calm, inward conviction of my union with good, my oneness with God.

I have a deep realization that I am surrounded by an infinite Law which receives the impress of my thought and acts creatively upon it.

I am conscious of my ability to use this Law, to direct it for specific purposes, for myself and others.

There is nothing in me that can deny, limit, obstruct, divert or in any way hinder my use of this Law.

There is no argument, no belief, no superstition, no doubt that can cast any shadow of unbelief across my mind.

I realize that this Law exists and I am conscious that I know how to use It.

It is certain that you will have to love your fellowman if you wish to be happy. Your union with God implies your union with everything that lives. Do not be afraid of this. Do not shun the thought of it. Divine union means union with everything. This does not mean that you love those who are closest to you any less; you merely love all humanity more.

Think for a moment about the few upon whom you have lavished particular affection. Now permit your imagination to include more. Say to yourself: "What would it be like if these few whom I love so much were multiplied so that finally everyone I meet should arouse in me the same deep affection?" Dare to lose your small affection and you will find it increased and multiplied a million times through greater union.

Learn to be at home in the universe. No more loneliness. No more sense of isolation. See God in everyone—the same God with a different face, the same animating Principle with a different form, the same Divine Presence clothed in individual expression. There is a fountain of life, from which, if a man drink, he shall never thirst again. Your search is after this fountain that you may be immersed in it. You cannot plunge into the waters of real Life unless you take everyone in with you. The universe is one system.

You cannot be happy unless you believe in immortality. You not only have the joy of living today, but an equal joy of knowing that you will live forever. Always your horizons will be expanding, forever filling your life with new hope, new vigor and new assurance.

You are an eternal being now on the pathway of endless unfoldment, never less but always more yourself. Life is not static. It is forever dynamic, forever creating—not something done and finished, but something alive, awake and aware. There is something within you that sings the song of eternity. Listen to it. There is an eternal springtime of your soul. Always rising but never setting is the sun of your destiny.

Commune with the invisible Presence within you until there comes a certainty which is beyond hope, something which enables you to see clear-eyed the future as you see the past. God grant that you shall enter into this freedom today. Say:

I refuse to worry about anything.

I have complete confidence that the God Who is always with me is able and willing to direct everything I do, to control my affairs, to lead me into the pathway of peace and happiness.

I free myself from every sense of condemnation, either against myself or others.

I loose every sense of animosity.

I now understand that there is a Principle and a Presence in every person gradually drawing him into the Kingdom of Good.

I know that the Kingdom of God is at hand, and I am resolved to enter into this Kingdom, to possess it, and to let it possess me.

You have a silent partner within you whose energy is inexhaustible and whose intelligence is without limit. Your silent partner is more than a subjective or unconscious reaction to life; it is Life Itself.

You must find and maintain a close communion with your true Center. Your creative power is not an act of the will. It is, rather, an act of your willingness to believe, and you are believing in something greater than your objective self, something deeper than your subconscious self, something beyond the collective thought of the world. Your creative power comes from the originating Spirit Itself, which knows no limit, is conditioned by no circumstance and governed by no law outside Itself.

Throw yourself with complete abandon into the all-consuming fire of inward conviction. Say:

I know that the Divine Spirit is operating through me now.

I know that I am not limited by anything that has happened, or by anything that   is   now   happening.

I am entering into an entirely new set of conditions and circumstances. That which has no limit is flowing through my consciousness into action.

I am guided by the same Intelligence and inspired by the same Imagination which scatters the moonbeams across the waves, and holds the forces of nature in Its grasp.

Try to feel such a close union with this invisible Presence that It becomes to you as an infinite Person—not a person separated from you, but the Person operating through you.

Unity does not mean uniformity. Therefore, you know that God is always acting in you in a unique way, in an original manner. Try to feel that every day something new and wonderful is going to happen to you. Say:

I am conscious that the Divine Spirit is acting through me.

I am aware that the Truth is making me free from any belief in want, lack or limitation.

There is no doubt or uncertainty in my mind.

I have a feeling of security and of ability to do anything that I should do.

I am not afraid of life or death, for I know that death is swallowed up in life.

I know that every living soul will find complete emancipation sooner or later. Therefore, I stand "amidst the eternal ways" and let the winds of God blow full and free around me.

You have just as much evidence of the existence of your soul as you do of the existence of an atom.

While it is true that no one has ever seen this soul, it is also true that no one has ever seen love, beauty or intelligence. You have an invisible body right now. You are as immortal now as you ever will become, and you should begin to live like an immortal being.

The soul is the one triumphant, indestructible and unconquerable thing you possess. Shot from the Invisible into this experience, it constitutes your great reality. But why wait for physical death to enjoy and experience your immortal being? Do not prepare to die. Prepare to live, whether you are ten years old or one hundred. There is no death. It is impossible for you to die. Stop trying to die and learn to live.

Each autumn brings its harvest, yet it never leaves you with a thought of finality. There will always be a new planting, new blossoms and new fruits, new seed times and new harvests. It makes no difference what your harvest may have been last year; today you can create a new future if you have the faith to believe that you can. Plant, then, new hopes and aspirations. The Lord of the harvest will permit you to reap what you have sown.

Chapter XIII

YOU KNOW that Life cannot withhold Itself from you. All that Life is and has is fully given to you to enjoy. The Life of God is perfect and eternal. It is the essence of everything that is. Life is God's gift to you. It is always ready to manifest Itself through you in Its entire fullness.

You are a self-choosing mind in a Divinity which permeates everything. You are always in the midst of Life, a Life that lives eternally and lives through you now. Therefore, you need not be disturbed by the passage of time, the movement around you, or the variations of experience through which you go. There is something within you that remains unmovable, that always speaks directly to you, saying, "Be still and know that I am God." Say:

Consciously, I draw upon the Life that is mine.

I know that the fullness of Life, which is Divine in Its origin, eternal in Its presence, and forever available, is mine.

The Life of the eternal Spirit is my life.

The infinite riches of Its being are mine to enjoy.

The vitality, the wisdom and the peace of God are mine.

I accept them in fullness, in joy and in peace.

You are part of the Universal Mind, one with the Universal Substance. You live, move and have your being in pure Spirit. All the wealth, the power and the goodness of this Spirit exist at the center of your being. You experience this good in such degree as you accept, believe in and feel it.

Since the only life you can have is the Life of the Spirit within you, you need but permit Its radiance to flow through your thought into self-expression. You are surrounded by a dynamic force, a great surge of living power. You are immersed in and saturated with the vital essence of Life. Its presence permeates everything, binding all together in one complete whole.

As you enter into life, feeling the Divine Presence in everything, more and more you will hear a Song of Joy singing at the center of your being. You have only to be still and listen to this Song of Life, for it is always there. Say:

Knowing that the loving Presence is always closer to me than my very breath, I have nothing to fear.

I feel this loving protection around me.

I know that the Song of Joy, of Love and of Peace, is forever chanting its hymn of praise and beauty at the center of my being, therefore, I tune out of my mind all unhappy and negative ideas.

Chapter XIII

I turn the dial of my thought into the sunshine of life, into brightness and laughter, into the joyous presence of radiant Spirit.

I lay aside all anxiety, all striving, and let the law of Divine Love operate through me into my affairs.

Joyfully I anticipate greater abundance, more success and a deeper peace.

Joy wells up within my mind and Life sings Its song of ecstasy in my heart.

The Chinese sage said that Tao (meaning Spirit) "produces everything, nourishes everything, and maintains everything." It flows through and is in all things, being all that is. There is nothing outside It. There is a spiritual Presence pervading the universe, welling up in your consciousness, always proclaiming Itself to be the source of your being. The enlightened ones of the ages have told you that your recognition of Life is God within you recognizing Himself in everything you do.

There is but one Presence in the universe. Since It is in and through everything, It must be in and through you. This Presence manifests Itself in and through all forms, all people, all conditions. This Presence is Life Itself. Its nature is love and givingness.

Negation may be an experience and a fact; it can never be an ultimate truth. Life cannot operate against itself. Always the negative is overcome by the positive. Good cannot fail to overcome evil. The meek alone shall inherit the earth. Finally, it will obliterate everything unlike itself, even as the sun dissolves the mist. Say:

I refuse to contemplate evil as a power.

I know that it will flee from me; it dissolves and disappears in the light of love.

I know that hate cannot exist where love is recognized.

I turn the searchlight of Truth upon every apparent evil in my experience.

This light dissolves every image of evil.

The manifestation of good is complete.

Love makes the way clear before me.

I am guided into an ever-widening experience of living.

My every thought and act is an expression of the goodness which flows from Life.

The Divine circulates through me automatically, freely.

Every atom of my being is animated by Its action.

I know that at all times I have a silent, invisible Partner walking with me, talking with me, operating through me.

Continuously, I keep my mind open to Its guidance, to Its inspiration and illumination.

You are either attracting or repelling according to your mental attitudes. You are either identifying yourself with lack or with abundance, with love and friendship or with indifference. You cannot keep from attracting into your experience that which corresponds to the sum total of your states of consciousness. This law of attraction and repulsion works automatically. It is like the law of reflection—the reflection corresponds to the image held before a mirror. Life is a mirror peopled with the forms of your own acceptance.

How careful, then, you should be to guard your thoughts, not only seeing to it that you keep them free from doubt and fear—accepting only the good— but, equally, you should consciously repel every thought which denies that good.

Knowing that the Law of Mind works automatically upon your thought, or that your thought works upon It, you may free yourself from the sense of personal responsibility, while, at the same time, remaining aware that even spiritual laws must be definitely used if they are to produce tangible results in your experience. Say:

I believe, with absolute conviction, that my word will not return unto me void.

I know that spiritual laws execute themselves just as do all other laws of nature.

I know that my word penetrates any unbelief in my mind, casts out fear, removes doubt, clears away obstacles, permitting that which is enduring, perfect and true to be realized.

I have complete faith and acceptance that all the statements I make will be carried out as I have believed.

I do everything with a sense of reliance upon the Law of Good; therefore, I know that my word shall not return unto me void.

I accept this word and rejoice in it.

I expect complete and perfect results from it.

I relax and let a Power greater than myself work for me, in me and through me.

There is a God Power at the center of every man's being, a Presence that knows neither lack, limitation nor fear, sickness, disquiet or imperfection. This Presence and Power is at the center of all people and all things. But because everyone is an individual, he can build a wall of negative thought between himself and this perfection. This makes it difficult for the true center to come to the surface.

When this happens, the mind becomes impressed only by its external environment, which declares that impoverishment and pain must necessarily accompany every man in his experience through life. This whole process is an activity of thought, either consciously or unconsciously entertained. The wall which keeps you from the greater good is built of mental blocks, cemented together by fear and unbelief, mixed in the mortar of negative experience.

Now you are to tear down this wall, to completely destroy it. The view which this wall obstructed is now seen in all its grandeur. The sun never really stopped shining and the River of Life forever flows. Having destroyed the barrier, you may sit on the banks of this river contemplating the beauty of nature, or you may bathe in its refreshing coolness.

Every man's experience is an attempt to merge his own being with this eternal river, not to the loss of his identity, but to the discovery of that self which has never wholly left its heaven. Like an echo from some unknown shore there is a voice seeking to be heard. Like clouds which obscure the mountain tops of vision, thoughts of fear and doubt obstruct the greater view. Say:

I know that there is a Presence and a perfect Law irresistibly drawing into my experience everything which makes life happy and worthwhile.

I know that friendship, love and happiness belong to me.

Nothing but good can go forth from me.

The good that I receive is but the completion of a circle, the fulfillment of my desire for all.

I no longer judge according to appearances, be they mental or physical.

I have placed my reliance in the Power, the Presence and the Perfection of God.

Therefore, I have dominion over all apparent evil.

I repudiate all its claims, cast out every fear of or belief in that which is not good, and exercise the dominion which by divine right belongs to me.

I know that freedom and joy are mine today.

This freedom and joy spontaneously express themselves in my experience.

There is nothing in me that can obstruct their passage.

I permit them to flow through me in all their wonder and might.

I am conscious of an Infinite Wisdom directing me.

Chapter XIII

Whatever I ought to know I shall know. Whatever I ought to do I shall do. Whatever belongs to me will come to me. I am compelled to recognize my good, to understand and accept it, and to act upon it.
Therefore, I declare that every step of my way is guided and guarded. With joy I enter into the fulfillment of life.

Chapter XIV

YOUR KINGDOM of God is at hand. You have already inherited everything that belongs to this kingdom. The riches, power, glory and might of this kingdom are yours today. You do not rob others by entering into the fullness of your kingdom of joy, your kingdom of abundance. You recognize that all people belong to the same kingdom. You are merely claiming for yourself what you would that the law of good should do unto all.

There is no law of human heredity imposed upon you. Evil has no history. Limitation has no past. That which is opposed to good has no future. The eternal now is forever filled with the presence of perfect life. You always have been, and forever will remain, a complete and perfect expression of the Eternal Mind, which is God, the living Spirit Almighty. Say:

Today I enter into the limitless variations of self-expression which the Divine Spirit projects into my experience.

Knowing that all experience is a play of Life upon Itself, the blossoming of love into self-expression, the coming forth of good into the joy of its own being, I enter into the game of living with joyful anticipation, with enthusiasm.

I play the game of life well and I enjoy it.

Today I enter into my Divine inheritance, shaking my thought clear from the belief that external conditions are imposed upon me.

I wait at the doorway of my expectation until my acceptance grants me the privilege of beholding His face forever more.

I shall not wait long, for today I expect to see His shining presence, I expect to don the "seamless robe" of Divine union.

Today is my day.

I let it live itself through me.

All nature is a living example, a continuous reminder, that there is a Spirit animating everything, a Presence defused, a Law governing, a Unity sustaining, a coordinating Will binding all together, a unifying Principle holding everything in place. Say:

I cleanse the windows of my mind, that it may become a mirror reflecting inspiration from the most High.

I do this, not with strenuous effort, but through quiet contemplation, through gently reaching and affirming an inward recognition.

Today I walk in the pathway of inspiration.

Chapter XIV

I know exactly what to do in every situation.

There is an inspiration within me which governs every act, every thought, with certainty, with conviction and in peace.

The key that unlocks the treasures of the kingdom of good is in my hand.

I unlock the doorway of my consciousness and gently open it that the Divine Presence may flood my whole being with light, illumine my being with Its radiant glow, and direct my footsteps into the pathway of peace and joy.

Every part of your body is made of pure substance. There is a spiritual body which cannot deteriorate. This spiritual body is already within you. As much of it appears as is recognized. It is the mind that makes this recognition. It is the mind that blocks or permits the emanation of this spiritual body through the physical form.

Spiritual perfection always responds to man's consciousness but it can respond only in such degree as he becomes aware. This awareness is an inward feeling of conviction, and, in a sense, a mental digestion of its meaning. Your mind digests ideas just as your body digests food. Spiritual, mental and physical laws are identical. Each produces a similar action and reaction on its own plane of being.

You already have a spiritual body, but your mind is not aware of this. Therefore, the mind automatically becomes a mirror reflecting either the inward perfection or the outward, apparent imperfection. It is because this inward perfection is so insistent that you maintain a physical body, but because you are an individual with volition, you can, as it were, hang a curtain between your physical life and its spiritual cause.

Spiritual realization helps to withdraw this curtain. Every statement you make about your body, or belief you hold about it, with deep feeling which causes the mind to accept Spirit as the substance of the body, tends to heal.

Say:

I realize that there is a Divine Presence at the center of my being.

I let this recognition flow through my entire consciousness.

I let it reach down into the very depths of my being.

I rejoice in this realization.

The perfect Life of God is in and through me, in every part of my being.

As the sun dissolves the mist, so my acceptance of Life dissolves all pain and discord.

I   am   free   because   the   Spirit   of   Life   in   me   is   perfect.

It remolds and recreates my body after the likeness of the Divine pattern of body which exists in the Mind of God.

Even now the living Spirit is flowing through me.

I open wide the doorway of my consciousness to Its influx.

I permit this physical body to receive the living Spirit in every action, function, cell and organ.

I know that my whole being manifests the life, love, peace, harmony, strength and joy of the Spirit which indwells me, which is my entire being.

I am now made vigorous and whole.
I possess the vitality of the Infinite.

I am strong and well.

The life of the Spirit is my life.

All of Its strength is my strength. Its power is my power. Its body is my body.

Every breath I draw is a breath of perfection, vitalizing, building and renewing every cell of my body.
Life fills all space and Spirit animates every form. It is this Spirit in you, as you, which is the true actor in everything you do, but since you are an individual, even the Spirit cannot make the gift of Life unless you accept it. Life may have given everything to you but only that which you accept is yours to use. Life makes things out of Itself through the simple and direct process of Itself becoming that which It makes. This is why it is written that the word of power, of life and action is in your own mouth—that is, in your thought.
Turning from every objective fact to the Divine which is within you, is turning from conditions to causes, to that realm of Absolute Being which, through self-knowingness, creates the forms which It projects and enters into the experience which It creates. Thus the Spirit comes to self-fulfillment in everything. Everything is alive with God, saturated with Divinity.
There are many who will doubt this. Only to those who have believed has the

proof come. The highest hope and aspiration of humanity have been built around the lives of those few who have believed. You are one of these. You do believe. Nothing can dim your faith. Nothing can dampen your ardor. Nothing can cause you to doubt.

Through the manifestation of the power that is within you, you can project any objective experience which you may legitimately desire. Be certain that you are accepting this, that you are living in joyous expectation of good, that you are accepting abundance. Be sure that you are animating your experience with the thought of plenty, that you are affirming that Divine Substance is forever flowing to you as supply. Say:

Today I recognize the abundance of life.

I animate everything in my experience with this idea.

I remember only the good.

I accept only the good.

I expect only the good.

This is all I experience.

I give thanks that this good is flowing in ever-increasing volume.

I say to my mind, there is good enough to go around.

I do not withhold that good from myself or others, but proclaim that spiritual substance is forever flowing to each and to all as daily supply.

You should become accustomed to the thought that you are a divine being. Everything is a part of one great Whole. Everything in nature is an individualization of one coordinating Life, one Law of being, and one Presence. The mind has become so filled with that which contradicts this that even the Truth has to await our recognition.

You must learn to become consciously aware of the Divine Presence and the Divine Power, the wholeness of Truth, of Love, of Reason and of a sound mind. Instead of dwelling on negative thoughts, cause your mind to dwell on peace and joy. Know that the power of the invisible Spirit is working in and through you now, at this very moment. Lay hold of this realization with complete certainty. Say:

I know that I am a perfect being now, living under perfect conditions today.

Knowing that good alone is real, I know that there is one Power which acts and reacts in my experience, in my body and in my thought.

I know that good alone has power either to act or react.

Everything that 1 do, say or think today shall be done, said or thought from this spiritual viewpoint—that God, Who is Life, is in everything.

Chapter XIV

I know that this recognition establishes the law of harmony in my experience, the law of prosperity, a sense of happiness, peace, health and joy.

Today I hold communion with this invisible Presence which peoples the world with the manifestations of Its life, Its light and Its love.

I withdraw the veil which hides my real self, and draw close to the Spirit in everything and in everyone.

I accept everything that belongs to this Spirit,

I claim everything that partakes of Its nature.

Few have completely recognized their God within. Only a few have prepared their minds to receive this truth with all its meaning, with all its power, majesty and might. Now you are one of these. You have decided to live as though this were true. A deep and abiding faith has come to you. Therefore, you are fortunate among men. Not that God has favored you above others; rather, you have chosen this path and you are going to walk in it.

Realizing that you may, in your ignorance, have been using the power of your mind negatively (not because you were evil but because of human ignorance, superstition and fear, which, to a certain degree, permeates every man's thought) you are not going to condemn yourself or anyone else because of this. If the light has come, the thing to do is to use it, forgetting the darkness. When the day of enlightenment dawns, the night of darkness disappears. The light did not contend against this darkness and the darkness could not contend against the light. Say:

Today I realize that my good is at hand.

Today I know that my Redeemer liveth in me.

He is not outside that I need go in search of Him.

He is not in the mountain, nor even in the temple, holy as it may be.

He is within me, now, today, this very moment, in this breath I draw, in the eternal now and the everlasting here.

The Spirit within me refreshes me.

I am saturated with the essence of Life.

My body is a vehicle for Its expression, my mind an instrument for Its thought.

Today I shall consciously commune with this Spirit, which is my Spirit; with this Life, which is my Life. I shall endeavor to feel this Presence as a living reality in my life.

I shall try to sense the same Spirit in everyone.

I shall see Him everywhere.

Chapter XIV

Chapter XV

THERE IS a truth which can set you free from fear, want, unhappiness and finally death itself. This truth is already within you. Nothing could be more wonderful than this. It is what you have been looking for but hardly dared believe.

No matter what the negations of yesterday may have been, your affirmations of today may rise triumphant over them. This is the highest hope ever placed before the vision of man's search for something that can make him whole. The evil of all your yesterdays can vanish into nothingness. If you can see beauty instead of ugliness, beauty will appear. Cease weeping over the mistakes of yesterday, and steadfastly beholding the face of the great and divine Reality, walk in that Light wherein there is no darkness. Say:

I know that every negative condition of the past is swept aside.

I refuse to see it or to think about it.

Yesterday is no longer here; tomorrow has not yet arrived.

Today is God's day.

God's day is my day.

Today, bright with hope and filled with promise, is mine.

Today my heart is without fear.

I have implicit confidence in the good, the enduring and the true.

Today I shall guard my thought and speech; I shall keep my consciousness steadfast with the realization that there is a spiritual Power upon which I may rely.

I shall turn resolutely to that Divine Source which knows no confusion, to that spiritual Center which knows no fear.

The Spirit is not afraid of anything; the Divine has no enemies; the Spirit knows no opposites.

Consciously, I draw close to my Divine Center, the Source of all that is; I feel the warmth of Its presence.

I enter into a faith made perfect through love and confidence, an assurance made complete by the abandonment of myself to good.

Acknowledging good in all my ways, desiring only the good for others, I rest in calm assurance.

I open my consciousness to the realization that all the Power and Presence there is clothes me in Its eternal embrace; that the Spirit forever imparts Its life to me.

I believe in myself because I believe in God.

I believe in my destiny because I know that the Law of Good is operating through me.

I have confidence in the future and enthusiastic expectation of good things to come.

Therefore, I accept the fullness of life this moment.

Anything you ask for in the nature of the Divine Life, which is love, truth, beauty, power, wisdom, goodness and peace, you have a right to expect to receive. But it is only as you let go of the lesser that you can take hold of the greater, only as you drop confusion that you can entertain peace, only as you transcend doubt and fear that you can be lifted up to the hilltops of the inner Life.

In asking, you must identify yourself with the greatness of the Spirit. This is the only way you can breathe this Almighty Power. Permit your consciousness, through faith, to rise to a greater and broader realization of that Divine Presence which is always delivering Itself to you.

Believing that the Divine Mind is ever present, that Divine Intelligence is ever available, open your consciousness to Its guidance. Keep your mind steadfast and loyal to the thought that you are governed by this Divine Intelligence. Feel that you are impelled to make right decisions, that you are compelled to act upon these decisions intelligently, and know that the Power that is with you cannot desert you. Say:

My knowledge that the great I Am is ever available gives me an increasing capacity to draw upon It and to become inwardly aware of the presence of Spirit.

Through the quiet contemplation of the omni-action of Spirit, I learn to look quietly and calmly upon every false condition, seeing through it to the other side of the invisible Reality which molds conditions and recreates all of my affairs after a more nearly Divine pattern.

With a penetrating spiritual vision I can dissipate the obstruction, remove the obstacle, dissolve the wrong condition.

Standing still, I can watch the sure salvation of the Law.

I now claim health instead of sickness, wealth instead of poverty, happiness instead of misery.

Every thought of fear or limitation is removed from my consciousness.

I know that my word transmutes every energy into constructive action, producing health, harmony, happiness and success.

I know there is something at the center of my being which is absolutely certain of itself.

It has complete assurance and it gives me complete assurance that all is well.

I maintain my position as a Divine Being here and now.

I know that in this consciousness of Reality is the supply for my every need — physical, mental or spiritual—and I accept that supply in deepest gratitude.

I am thankful that this is the way Life fulfills my needs, through the doorway of my inner self, and I am thankful that I know how to use this perfect Law.

I come to this great Fountain of Supply, in the very center of my being, to absorb that for which I have need, mentally and physically, and I am filled with the sense of the Reality of that which I desire.

As I am filled with Reality I permit It to flow into my world of thought and action, knowing that It brings peace, harmony and order all around me.

There arises within me limitless faith in the unconquerable Presence, the perfect Law, and Divine Action.

Good is at the root of everything, regardless of its seeming absence. But this good must be recognized. Since there is but one Spirit and this Spirit is in you and in everything, then everywhere you go you will meet this Spirit. You meet this Spirit in people, in places and in things. There is a Divine Essence permeating everything, flowing through everything, becoming all things. This one Spirit, which manifests Itself in and through all, including yourself, automatically adjusts parts to the whole. Therefore, you may accept with positive certainty that the Spirit within you does go before you and prepares your way.

This is no idle conclusion, no empty dream, no forlorn hope. Your faith is placed in something positive, certain as the laws of life, exact as the principle of mathematics, ever present, like the ethers of space, ever operating like the laws of nature. Say:

I know that the Spirit within me goes before me, making perfect, plain, straight, easy and happy the pathway of my experience.

There is nothing in me that can obstruct the divine circuits of Life, of Love, of Beauty and Truth.

My word dissolves every negative thought or impulse that would throw a shadow of unbelief across the threshold of my expectation.

Today I have faith that my word shall not return unto me void.

I surrender myself completely to this faith.

My prayer, then, is one of affirmation and acceptance.

I lift my cup of acceptance, knowing that the Divine outpouring will fill it to the brim.

Chapter XV

Today I consciously identify myself with everything that belongs to goodness, truth and beauty.

I identify myself with abundance and success.

I identify myself with the Living Spirit—with all the power, all the presence and all the life there is.

Realizing that all action starts in and is a result of consciousness, prepare your mind to receive the best that life has to offer. Become increasingly aware of the one Presence, the one Life and the one Spirit, which is God. Try to drop all sense of lack or limitation from your thought.

Knowing that your word of truth is the Law of God in you, and believing that this Law is perfect, you must become consciously aware that It is operating in your affairs. The Spirit works for you through your belief. All things are possible to this Spirit, therefore, everything is possible to you in such degree as you can believe in and accept the operation of Spirit in your life.

There is something within you which is completely aware of its oneness with power, of its unity with life. Loose all thoughts of discord and fear, and permit the true pattern to come to the surface. Remember that thought patterns are acquired; therefore, the mind that accepted them can reject them.

No doubt most of these patterns are unconsciously taken into the mind. This makes no difference at all. What is there you can consciously loose, drop it out of your thought, refuse to think about it, refuse to feed it with the fire of imagination and feeling. Having nothing to live on, it will shrivel up and disappear. It is only the thought that is nourished that grows. The weeds are no longer there when they are pulled up, and the place where they were forgets that they ever have been. Say:

I allow the Divine Wholeness to flow through me in ever-widening circles of activity.

Every good I have experienced is now increased.

Every joy that has come into my life is now multiplied.

There is a new influx of inspiration into my thought.

I see more clearly than ever before that my divine birthright is freedom, joy and eternal goodness.

I realize that this same birthright is bequeathed to all people.

I rejoice that everyone has this common good.

The Divine Presence interprets Itself to me through love and friendship, through peace and harmony.

Knowing that life gives according to my faith, I lift my mind, I elevate my faith; I listen deeply to the song of my being.

Chapter XV

You have been told that all things are possible to him who believes. Accepting this as a principle of your being and analyzing it to its logical conclusion, you have come to understand that faith is not a nebulous something; it is an actual idea, a definite mental attitude, a positive acceptance—not positive from the standpoint of will power or compelling things to happen, not positive from the standpoint of influencing people or things, not positive from the standpoint of holding thoughts with ever tightening grip. Your faith is positive when that which your intellect announces is no longer denied by the accumulated patterns of thought held in the subconscious part of your mind.

Faith is most certainly a mental attitude. Faith is more than an objective statement; perfect faith cannot exist while there are subjective contradictions that deny the affirmation of the lips. It is only when the intellect is no longer obstructed by negative emotional reactions, arising out of the experiences of doubt and fear, that the word of the mouth can immediately bear fruit. There is nothing in this thought to be discouraged about, for the very fact that thoughts are things also carries with it this divine connotation that the thinker can change his thoughts, that he really is the master of his fate.

You are the thinker. You are the creator of thought patterns. You are the master of your fate. But you must exercise this mastership. Say:

I believe with a deep, inward calm that my word of faith is the execution of spiritual Law in my life.

I know that my word penetrates any and every unbelief in my thought; it casts out fear, removes doubts, and permits that which is enduring, perfect and true to enter into my consciousness.

I have complete conviction that my thoughts are not only true, but that they will be carried out in my experience with mathematical certainty.

I have absolute reliance upon the Law of Good.

I know that the Spirit, which is Life, is present everywhere.

Like the air I breathe, It presses against me; on the mountain top, in the valley, the desert and on the ocean, It is ever present.

I accept this Presence with complete confidence.

I believe that the Law of Good will bring everything desirable into my experience.

Today I proclaim my divine inheritance.

I am rich with the richness of God.

I am strong with the power of God.

I am guided by the wisdom of God.

I am held in the goodness of God, today.

The Spirit of God is an undivided and indivisible Wholeness. It fills all time with Its presence and peoples space with the activity of Its thought. It is, of course, difficult for the human mind to understand the meaning of such an all-encompassing Presence. However, perhaps the greatest difficulty is that we try to make it too abstract.

You already know that you live. You know that your life is peopled with events, persons coming and going, happenings that take place in your everyday experience, the thoughts in your own mind, the activities of your own affairs, the circulation of blood in your body. Don't you think this is the place to begin? You already understand the presence of life. It is not difficult, after all.

Your endeavor, then, is not so much to find God as it is to realize His Presence and to understand that this Presence is always with you. Nothing can be nearer to you than that which is the very essence of your being. Your outward search for God culminates in the greatest of all possible discoveries —the finding of Him at the center of your own being. Life flows up from within you. Say:

I know that my search is over.

I am consciously aware of the Presence of the Spirit.

I have discovered the great Reality.

I am awake to the realization of this Presence.

There is but one Life.

Today I see It reflected in every form, back of every countenance, moving through every act.

Knowing that the Divine Presence is in everyone I meet, the Spirit in all people, I salute the good in everything.

I recognize the God Life responding to me from every person I meet, in every event that transpires, in every circumstance in my experience.

I feel the warmth and color of this Divine Presence forevermore pressing against me, forevermore wetting up from within me—the wellspring of eternal being present yesterday, today, tomorrow, and always.

Did you ever stop to realize that peace must actually exist at the center of everything? And if you ask yourself, Why? Answer your own question, because in the long run you will have to do this anyway. No one can answer your questions for you but yourself. Your very nature has willed it so. Peace must exist at the center of everything or the universe itself would be a chaos. You already know this and believe it; now you are going to act upon it.

Chapter XV

You are not only going to believe in it, you are going to act as though it were true, because it is true. There is peace at the center of your being—a peace that can be felt throughout the day and in the cool of the evening when you have turned from your labor and the first star shines in the soft light of the sky. It broods over the earth quietly, tenderly, as a mother watches over her child. Say:

In this peace that holds me so gently I find strength and protection from all fear or anxiety.

It is the peace of God in which I feel the love of a Holy Presence.

I am so conscious of this love, this protection, that every sense of fear slips away from me as mist fades in the morning light.

I see good in everything, God personified in all people, Life manifest in every event.

Today you are to identify yourself with the more abundant life, to think on those things which make for peace, to dwell on the unity which underlies everything. As you consciously poise yourself in the realization that you live in pure Spirit, new power will be born within you. You will find yourself renewed by the Divine Life, led by Divine Intelligence and guarded by Divine Love. Focus your inward vision on this indwelling harmony, knowing that as you contemplate its perfection you will see it manifest in everything you do. Say:

Realizing that the Spirit within me is God, the Living Spirit Almighty, being fully conscious of this Divine Presence as the sustaining Principle of my life, I open my thought to Its influx.

I open my consciousness to Its outpouring.

This is the Mind of Truth, the Mind of God, carrying with It all the power of the Infinite. I know and understand that Good alone is real.

I know that silently I am drawing into my experience today, and every day, an ever-increasing measure of truth and beauty, of goodness and harmony.

Everything I do, say and think is quickened into right action, into productive action, into increased action.

My invisible good already exists.

My faith, drawing upon this invisible good, causes that which was unseen, to become visible.

All there is, is mine NOW; all there ever was or ever can be, is mine NOW.

Chapter XV

Chapter XVI

THE LAW of the Lord is perfect, and the law of the Lord is love. You are made perfect in the law when you enter into conscious communion with the love. Love is the fulfillment of the law; that is, it is only through love that the law can fulfill itself in your experience, because love harmonizes everything, unifies everything. It gives to everything, flows through everything. You can never make the most perfect use of the law of your life unless that use is motivated by love.

As the artist weds himself to beauty, imbibing the essence or spirit of beauty that it may be transmitted to the canvas or awaken the cold marble to living form, so you must wed yourself to love. You must imbibe its spirit. This love is more than a sentiment. It is a deep sense of the underlying unity and beauty of all life, the goodness running through everything, the givingness of Life to everything. Say:

Today I bestow the essence of Love upon everything.

Everyone shall be lovely to me.

My soul meets the soul of the universe in everyone.

Everything is beautiful; everything is meaningful.

This Love is a healing power touching everything into wholeness, healing the wounds of experience with its divine balm.

I know that this Love Essence is the very Substance of Life, the creative Principle back of everything, flowing through my whole being, spiritual, emotional, mental and physical.

It flows in transcendent loveliness into my world of thought and form, ever renewing, vitalizing, bringing joy, harmony and blessing to everything and everyone it touches.

You are to know that good keeps you in perfect activity, surrounds you with love and friendship, and brings the experience of joy to everything you do. You are to impart an atmosphere of confidence and faith which uplifts and enlightens everything in your environment. It is only as you live affirmatively that you can be happy. Knowing that there is but one Spirit in which everyone lives, moves and has his being; you are to feel this Spirit not only in your consciousness but in your affairs. You are to hold conscious communion with this Spirit in humanity. In a handclasp you can feel Its warmth and color. In the exchange of thought you are to feel the Presence of the Divine. You are to sense It in everything.

You are united with all. You are one with the eternal Light Itself. The

Presence of Spirit within you blesses everyone you meet, tends to heal everything you touch, brings gladness into the life of everyone you contact. Therefore, you are a blessing to yourself, to mankind and to the day in which you live. Say:

Today I uncover the perfection within me. In its fullness I reveal the indwelling Kingdom.

I look out upon the world of my affairs, knowing that the Spirit within me makes my way both immediate and easy.

I know there is nothing in me that could possibly obstruct or withhold the divine circuit of Life and Love, which Good is.

My word dissolves every negative thought or impulse that could throw a shadow over my perfection.

Good flows through me to all.

Good shines through my thoughts and actions.

Good harmonizes my body, so that it is revitalized and manifests perfection in every cell, in every organ, in every function.

Good harmonizes my mind, so that Love sings joyously in my heart.

I am completely conscious of All-Good in me, around me and in all that is.

I am in complete unity with Good.

I have complete confidence in my knowledge and understanding of the Law of Good.

I not only know what the Law is, I know how to use It. I know that I shall obtain definite results through the use of It.

I realize that doubts about my ability to use this Law are things of thought. What thought has produced, thought can change.

Knowing this, having confidence in my ability to use the Law, and using It daily for specific purposes, gradually I build up an unshakable faith, both in the Law and the possibility of demonstrating It.

There is no doubt in me, no uncertainty rising through me. My mind rejoices in certainty and in assurance.

I confidently expect that my word shall not return unto me void.

Therefore, today I declare that the Law of the Lord is perfect in everything I do.

Chapter XVI

It will externalize happiness, It will bring every good thing to me.

Today I am inwardly aware that there is a secret way of the soul, there is a secret pathway of peace, there is an invisible Presence forever externalizing Itself for me and through me.

Today I believe in Divine Guidance.

Today I rest in this divine assurance and this divine security.

I know, not only that all is well with my soul, my spirit and my mind—all is well with my affairs.

You live in the house of God. The household of God is a household of perfection. It is "the secret place of the most high" within you and within all. The inmates of this household are all divine. They will become as divine to you as you permit. As you look at them they look at you, for this is the way of life. Everything responds to you at the level of your recognition of it.
In the household of God there is no jealousy, no littleness nor meanness. It is a household of joy, a place of happiness and contentment. Here is warmth, color and beauty. Seen in this light, your earthly house symbolizes the Kingdom of Divine Harmony in which no one is a stranger. Say:
Nothing is alien to me.
Nothing enters into my experience but joy, integrity and friendship.
The good I would realize for myself I realize for all others.
I cannot desire a good for myself other than the good I desire for everyone else.
Neither do I deny myself the good I affirm for others.
I know that in the household in which I live the host is God, the living Spirit Almighty; the guests are all people; the invitation has been eternally written for all to enter and dwell therein as the, guests of this Eternal Host forever.
Life has set the stamp of individuality on your soul. You are different from any other person who ever lived. You are an individualized center in the Consciousness of God. You are an individualized activity in the Action of God. You are you, and you are eternal. Therefore, do not wait for immortality. The resurrection of life is today. You are clothed with this resurrection now. All you need to do is to experience it.
Begin to live today as though you are an immortal being and all thought of

95

death, all fear of change will slip from you. You will step out of the tomb of uncertainty into the light of eternal day. The nighttime of your soul will have passed and the eternal light of everlasting day will dawn as the great reality in your life. Say:

The perfect Law of Good is operating through me. Joyfully I accept It.

Joyfully I permit Its action in everything that I do.

I know that my recognition of good is the substance of the good which I recognize, and I know that this good is ever taking form in my experience.

It is impossible for me to be separated from my good.

Today, realizing that there is nothing in my past which can rise against me, nothing in my future which can menace the unfoldment of my experience, life shall be an eternal adventure, an unfolding experience of greater and better experiences.

Today I exult in this abundant life.

I revel in the contemplation of the immeasurable future, the path of eternal progress, the everlastingness of my own being, the ongoing of my soul, the daily renewed energy and action of that Divinity within me, which has forever set the stamp of individualized Being on my mind.

Surely, God has imparted Himself to every soul. If this were not true you would not be alive, you would have no existence, you could not be here. This living Presence is at the center of your being now, not by and by. If you open the door of your consciousness and welcome this Divine Guest, He will enter. Not a person lives who does not at some time in his life sense this inward Presence, this vision of the Divine which presses against us. It is seeking entrance through our thoughts. We must open the door of our consciousness and permit It to enter.

We do not will this Presence into existence, nor do we by declaration, affirmation or demand, command It. We do not court It through false humility nor engage Its attention by admiration. The Presence, the Power, is already there. It is willingness, acceptance and recognition which give entrance to the Divine Presence. It is faith and acknowledgment which permit Its creative power to flow through our word. Say:

Today I realize that the Spirit incarnated in me, God as my own being, constitutes the only reality I have.

I know that He dwells in me and I know that there is an invisible Guide, a living Presence with me at all times.

With complete simplicity and directness, I recognize my Divine center.

There is one Life in and through all. Consciously, I unify myself with this pure Spirit in which I live, move and have my being.

I am strong with the strength of the all-vitalizing power of pure Spirit.

I am sustained by Divine Energy which flows through me as radiant health and vitality.

Every atom of my being responds to this Divine Presence.

I completely surrender myself to It.

Everyone seeks the protecting power of some Presence which is close enough to reach out and take hold of. As a child turns to its parents for comfort, so every man is relying on God, whether or not he realizes it. This concept is so universal that it has been present in every age, with all people, and at all times. It would be a mockery of faith to deny that such a Presence exists or that such a Power operates.

All who have found an answer to life have believed in this. All who have wrought great and mighty works through faith have had complete confidence in this Divine Presence, and the greatest souls have known that this Presence is within. With equal confidence you should believe in the protecting Presence of the ever-available Spirit. With equal faith you should wrap yourself in a mantle of Divine protection.

Today you are to hold your thought steadfast in the realization that God withholds nothing from you. Therefore, prepare yourself for a life of joy, love, happiness and well-being. Believe in the Divine freedom which is yours by birthright. Say:

I know that the Law of God surrounds me with love and friendship.

I permit this love and friendship to flow out to all things, to all people, everywhere.

I let it radiate in my environment, bless everything I touch, make whole that which is weak, turn fear into faith, and accomplish the miracle of healing through love. Whatsoever things are good and true, I shall think upon.

This I shall remember—that the Spirit is not far off.

I shall remind myself that I live in the Divine Presence, that my affairs are in the keeping of the Eternal Mind.

I live, move and have my being in Wholeness.

Peace, poise and power belong to my Kingdom.

I give joy and love to all, knowing that the gift of Life is not to me alone.

I share my good.

I welcome the opportunity to love fully, completely and joyfully.

I believe in myself because I believe in God.

Chapter XVI

I accept life fully, completely, without reservation, holding to the conviction that good is the eternal Reality, that God is the everlasting Presence, is the eternal Guide, that my life is complete today.

We Have Book Recommendations for You

- The Strangest Secret by Earl Nightingale (AUDIOBOOK and Paperback)

- Acres of Diamonds (MP3 AUDIO) [UNABRIDGED] by Russell H. Conwell

- Think and Grow Rich [MP3 AUDIO] [UNABRIDGED]
  by Napoleon Hill, Jason McCoy (Narrator)

- As a Man Thinketh [UNABRIDGED]
  by James Allen, Jason McCoy (Narrator) (Audio CD)

- Your Invisible Power: How to Attain Your Desires by Letting Your Subconscious Mind Work for You [MP3 AUDIO] [UNABRIDGED]

- Thought Vibration or the Law of Attraction in the Thought World [MP3 AUDIO] [UNABRIDGED]
  by William Walker Atkinson, Jason McCoy (Narrator)

- The Law of Success - Napoleon Hill [MP3 AUDIO]

- The Law of Success, Volumes II & III: A Definite Chief Aim & Self -Confidence by Napoleon Hill (Paperback)

- Thought Vibration or the Law of Attraction in the Thought World & Your Invisible Power (Paperback)

- Automatic Wealth, The Secrets of the Millionaire Mind - Including: As a Man Thinketh, The Science of Getting Rich, The Way to Wealth and Think and Grow Rich (Paperback)

ONLINE AT:
www.bnpublishing.com

Printed in the United States
123672LV00001B/310-333/A